# THE BATMAN ADVENTURES

## VOLUME 2

# THE BATMAN ADVENTURES

## VOLUME 2


KELLEY PUCKETT
writer

MIKE PAROBECK
penciller

RICK BURCHETT
inker

RICK TAYLOR
colorist

TIM HARKINS
STARKINGS/COMICRAFT
letterers

RICK BURCHETT
collection cover artist


BATMAN created by BOB KANE

| | |
|---|---|
| Scott Peterson | Editor—Original Series |
| Darren Vincenzo | Assistant Editor—Original Series |
| Jeb Woodard | Editor |
| Robbin Brosterman | Design Director—Books |
| Sarabeth Kett | Publication Design |
| | |
| Bob Harras | Senior VP—Editor-in-Chief, DC Comics |
| | |
| Diane Nelson | President |
| Dan DiDio and Jim Lee | Co-Publishers |
| Geoff Johns | Chief Creative Officer |
| Amit Desai | Senior VP—Marketing & Franchise Management |
| Amy Genkins | Senior VP—Business & Legal Affairs |
| Nairi Gardiner | Senior VP—Finance |
| Jeff Boison | VP—Publishing Planning |
| Mark Chiarello | VP—Art Direction & Design |
| John Cunningham | VP—Marketing |
| Terri Cunningham | VP—Editorial Administration |
| Larry Ganem | VP—Talent Relations & Services |
| Alison Gill | Senior VP—Manufacturing & Operations |
| Hank Kanalz | Senior VP—Vertigo & Integrated Publishing |
| Jay Kogan | VP—Business & Legal Affairs, Publishing |
| Jack Mahan | VP—Business Affairs, Talent |
| Nick Napolitano | VP—Manufacturing Administration |
| Sue Pohja | VP—Book Sales |
| Fred Ruiz | VP—Manufacturing Operations |
| Courtney Simmons | Senior VP—Publicity |
| Bob Wayne | Senior VP—Sales |

BATMAN ADVENTURES VOLUME 2



DC Comics, 4000 Warner Blvd., Burbank, CA 91522
A Warner Bros. Entertainment Company.
Printed by RR Donnelley, Salem, VA, USA. 4/24/15 First Printing.
ISBN: 978-1-4012-5463-6

Library of Congress Cataloging-in-Publication Data

Puckett, Kelley.
Batman Adventures Volume 2 / Kelley Puckett, writer ; Mike Parobeck, artist.
pages cm

ISBN 978-1-4012-5463-6 (paperback)
1. Graphic novels. I. Parobeck, Mike, illustrator. II. Title.

PN6728.B36P773 2014
741.5'973—dc23

2014033208

Certified Sourcing
www.sfiprogram.org
SFI-01042
APPLIES TO TEXT STOCK ONLY

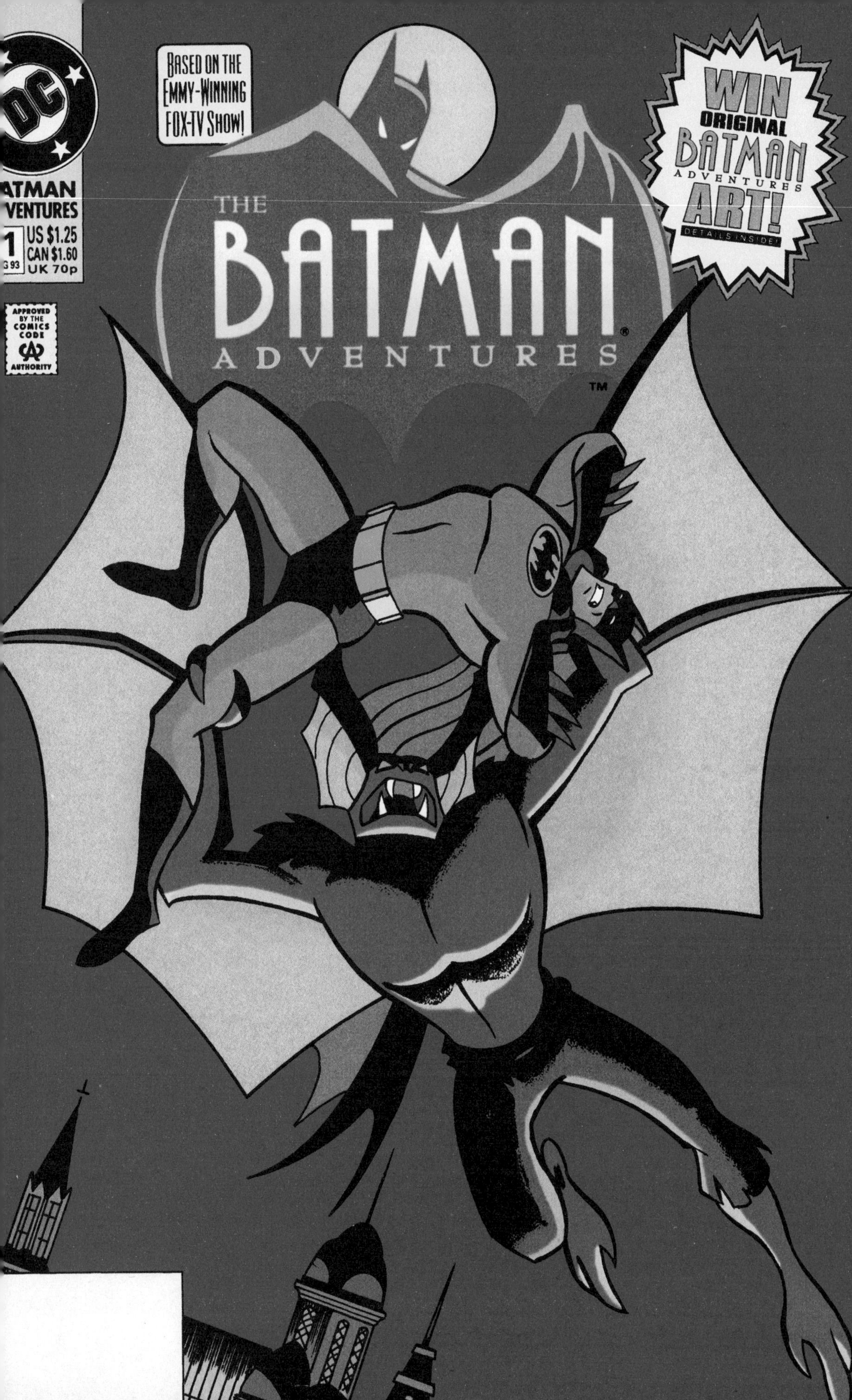
DC
BATMAN
ADVENTURES
1
US $1.25
CAN $1.60
UK 70p
APPROVED BY THE COMICS CODE AUTHORITY
BASED ON THE EMMY-WINNING FOX-TV SHOW!
THE BATMAN ADVENTURES
TM
WIN ORIGINAL BATMAN ADVENTURES ART!
DETAILS INSIDE!

THE BEAST WITHIN!
unh
ACT ONE: THE SLEEPER AWAKENS!
KELLEY PUCKETT WRITER
MIKE PAROBECK PENCILLER
RICK BURCHETT INKER
RICK TAYLOR COLORIST
TIM HARKINS LETTERER
SCOTT PETERSON EDITOR
Batman Created by BOB KANE

...FOR HIS CONTINUED EXCELLENCE IN THE FIELD OF BIONOMICS, THIS AWARD GOES TO DR. KIRK LANGSTROM.
BRUCE, THIS IS WONDERFUL! I HAD NO IDEA YOU WERE INTERESTED IN SCIENCE.
I'M NOT, BUT THE FREE PUBLICITY IS GREAT FOR MY IMAGE.
CLAP CLAP CLAP
OF COURSE. SILLY ME.
ACCEPTING THE AWARD FOR DR. LANGSTROM IS HIS WIFE, DR. FRANCINE LANGSTROM.
EXCELLEN
THANK YOU. I DON'T OFTEN GET TO BRAG ABOUT MY HUSBAND IN FRONT OF SUCH A LARGE CROWD.
2

I'M SORRY HE COULDN'T BE HERE HIMSELF, BUT HE'S IN THE LAB EVEN NOW, CONTINUING THE BOLD RESEARCH YOU'VE HONORED HIM FOR...
oh no.
IT'S A MONSTER!
AAA!!!!EEE!
LADIES AND GENTLEMEN! DON'T PANIC!
MY GOD!
3

WHOOOOOSSH
RUN!
KRASSHH
GRARRRRRR

AKK--
ARRRGH!
NNNK
Modak Film
Cola
5

GAUCHO
FOR MEN
WHHAAAAAM!!
6

KIRK!
OH, KIRK. WHY DID YOU DO IT? WHY?
KIRK, WAKE UP! THEY'LL BE COMING FOR YOU! WE'VE GOT TO GET OUT OF HERE!
7

# ACT 2: G.C.P.D.H.Q.!

GOTHAM CITY POLICE

POLICE

THAT WAS HIS WIFE, *HUH*?

HOW COME THE *CRAZIES* GET ALL THE WOMEN? EXPLAIN THAT TO ME.

YOU CAN'T IMAGINE WHAT IT'S LIKE, BATMAN. TO SOAR THROUGH THE SKY, TO HAVE THE STRENGTH OF TEN MEN, TO BE CAPABLE OF ANYTHING...
...AND TO KNOW FOR THE REST OF YOUR LIFE THAT YOU'RE ONLY AN HOUR AWAY FROM HAVING IT ALL AGAIN.
I USED TO THINK ABOUT IT CONSTANTLY. THE ONLY THING THAT COULD DISTRACT ME FROM IT WAS MY WORK. THAT...
...AND FRANCINE.
PLEASE, BATMAN, I'D... LIKE TO BE ALONE NOW.
9

DR. STEFAN PARRY. I'M HERE TO SEE THE PRISONER.
YOU GOT ANOTHER VISITOR, LANGSTROM.
STEFAN...?
HUH?
WHAT WAS THAT?
GOTHAM CITY POLICE
9765

HE'S GOT DR. PARRY!
WWHHHHAAAAM
AAAHHH!
WHHOOOSH
uhh
OH MY GOD!
HEY, YOU!
11

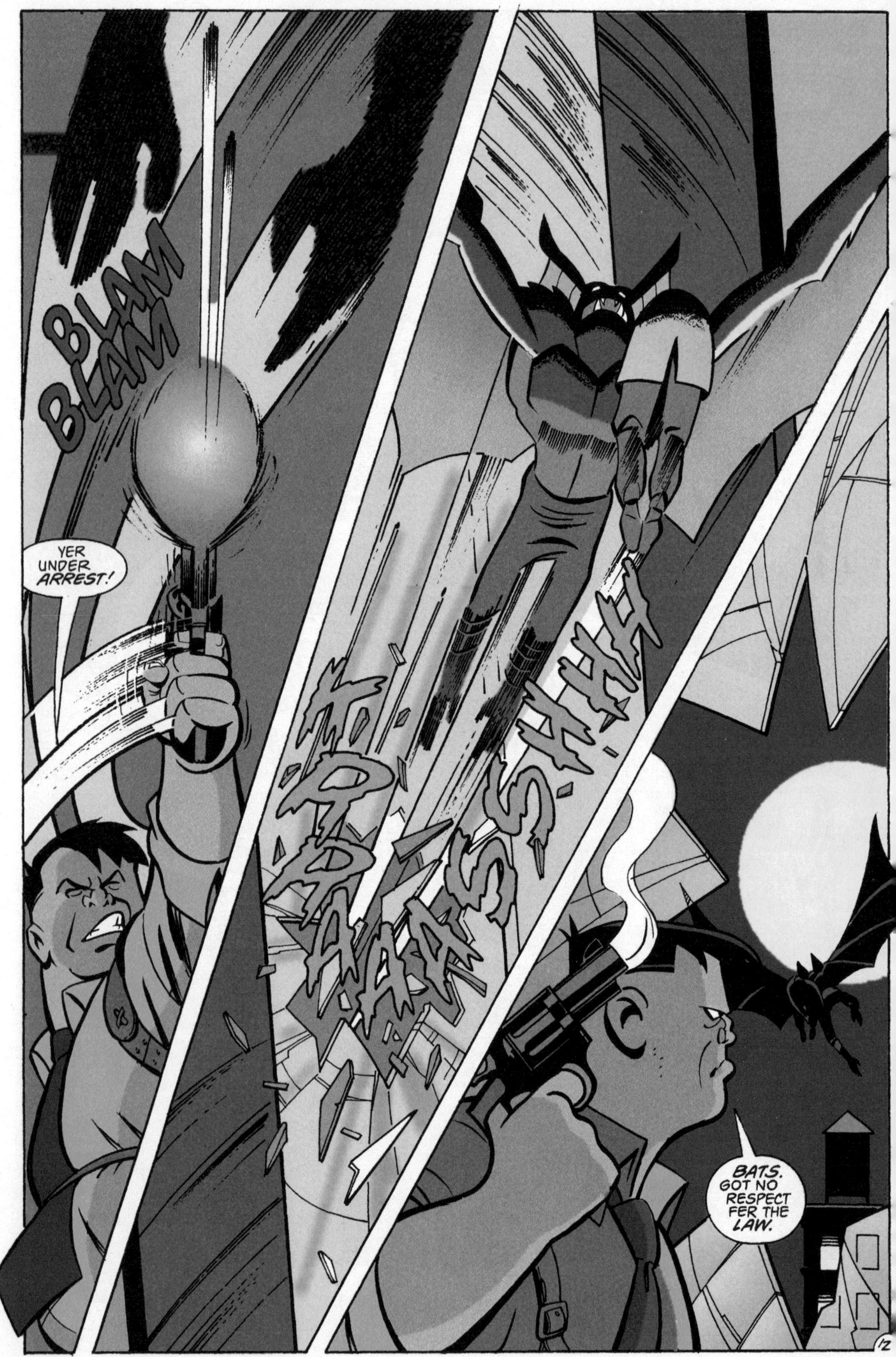
BLAM
BLAM
YER UNDER ARREST!
KRRAASSHH
BATS. GOT NO RESPECT FER THE LAW.
12

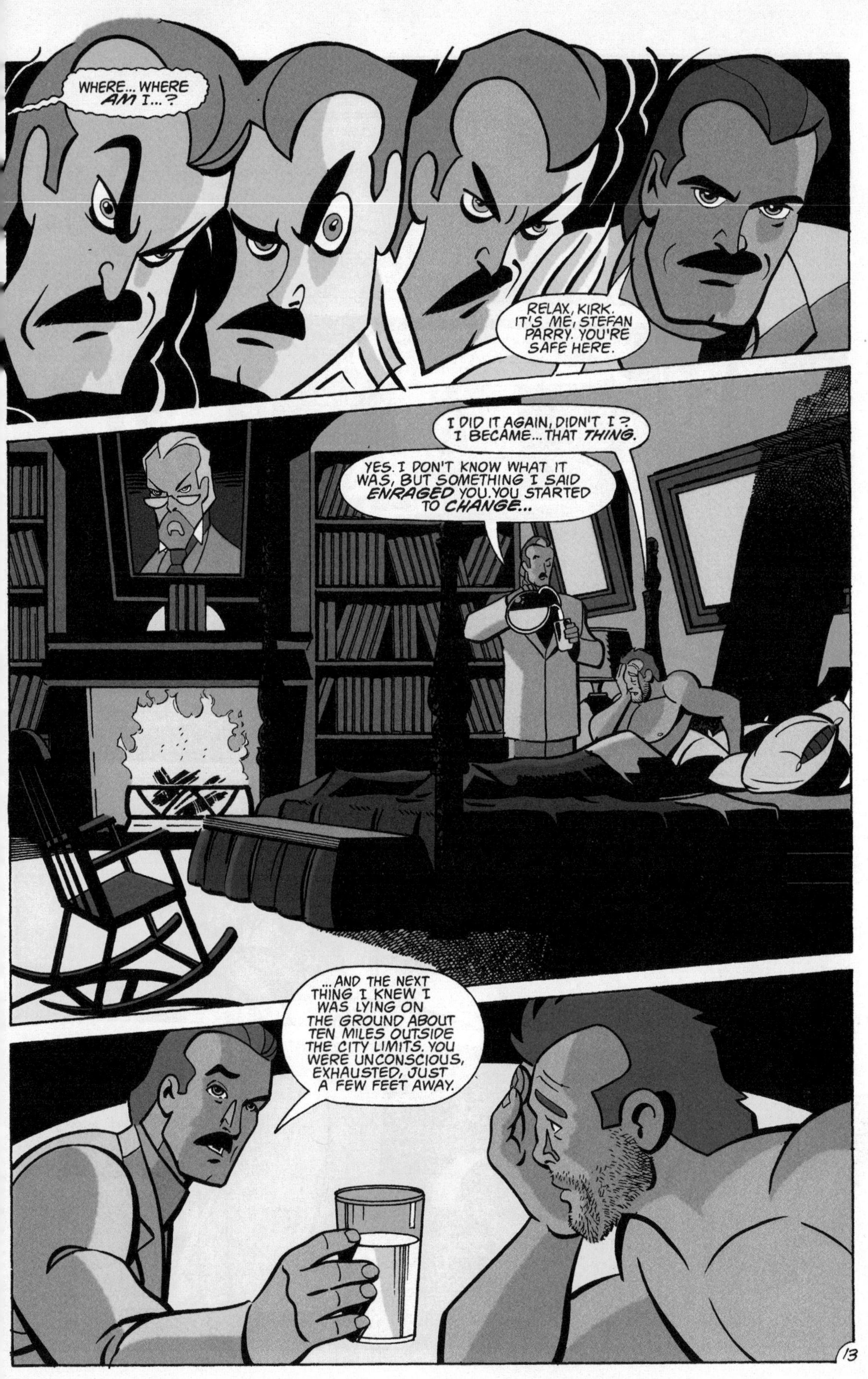
WHERE... WHERE AM I...?
RELAX, KIRK. IT'S ME, STEFAN PARRY. YOU'RE SAFE HERE.
I DID IT AGAIN, DIDN'T I? I BECAME... THAT THING.
YES. I DON'T KNOW WHAT IT WAS, BUT SOMETHING I SAID ENRAGED YOU. YOU STARTED TO CHANGE...
...AND THE NEXT THING I KNEW I WAS LYING ON THE GROUND ABOUT TEN MILES OUTSIDE THE CITY LIMITS. YOU WERE UNCONSCIOUS, EXHAUSTED, JUST A FEW FEET AWAY.
13

I BROUGHT YOU BACK HERE. YOU'VE BEEN ASLEEP FOR THE LAST SIXTEEN HOURS.
SIXTEEN HOURS? WHAT ABOUT THE POLICE?

OH, THEY'VE COME AND GONE ALREADY. I MADE UP A STORY AND SENT THEM ON THEIR WAY.
BUT... WHY DID YOU DO ALL THIS?

I CAN HELP YOU, KIRK. WORKING TOGETHER, WE'LL FIND A WAY TO RID YOU OF THAT HORRIBLE MUTAGEN PERMANENTLY.
I... DON'T KNOW WHAT TO SAY...

I'D ALWAYS THOUGHT ...YOU RESENTED ME ALL THESE YEARS... BECAUSE I WON THAT SCHOLARSHIP...
SLEEP WELL, LANGSTROM.
14

# ACT THREE: THE AWFUL TRUTH!

...BUT AFTER SEEING YOUR LAB SETUP HERE, IT'S ALL BECOME CLEAR. TELL ME WHERE LANGSTROM IS AND LET'S END THIS.
YOU KNOW I CAN'T DO THAT. I'M GOING TO COUNT TO THREE, BATMAN...
BATMAN! WAIT!
I'M GIVING MYSELF UP. I'M TOO DANGEROUS NOW, I REALIZE THAT. BUT STEFAN WAS JUST TRYING TO HELP ME. PLEASE LEAVE HIM OUT OF THIS.
LANGSTROM! GET OUT OF THE WAY...
16

YOU STILL DON'T GET IT, DO YOU? THAT SCHOLARSHIP SHOULD HAVE BEEN MINE! FOR TEN YEARS I'VE WAITED FOR MY CHANCE AT REVENGE!
I ALTERED YOUR MAN-BAT FORMULA TO WORK ON MY METABOLISM! I KNOCKED YOU OUT, TRANSFORMED MYSELF, AND FRAMED YOU FOR MY WRECKING SPREE.
BUT ONCE I'D EXPERIENCED ALL THAT POWER, I HAD TO HAVE IT AGAIN. SO I ARRANGED YOUR "BREAK-OUT"-- TRANSFORMING IN YOUR CELL AND DISGUISING YOU WITH MY LAB COAT.
NOW THAT YOU'RE "AT LARGE," I CAN CONTINUE AS MAN-BAT INDEFINITELY!
AND ON THAT NOTE, GENTLEMEN...
17

KKRRRAAASSHK
RRRUH?
WWWHHAAAMMMM!
18

PARRY HAS TO KNOW WHERE KIRK IS. HE HAS TO!
KIRK! NO!
WWWHHAAAAAMMM!!
KIRK!
19

FLY AWAY, QUICKLY! YOU'VE GOT TO GO!

KIRK? KIRK, IT'S ME? IT'S ME, KIRK! KIRK!

GROWRRR

THWAP
GRRRRRR
UGK
THOK
NOOOO!
UGHHHRRRRR
21

PARRY?

IT WASN'T ME, DARLING. IT WAS NEVER ME.
BUT I THOUGHT... I THOUGHT YOU'D...

IT'S OVER, LANGSTROM.

IS IT, BATMAN?
The End

WIN ORIGINAL BATMAN ADVENTURES ART!
DETAILS INSIDE!
APPROVED BY THE COMICS CODE AUTHORITY
DC
US $1.25
CAN $1.60
UK 70p
FOX KIDS NETWORK
THE BATGIRL ADVENTURES
TM

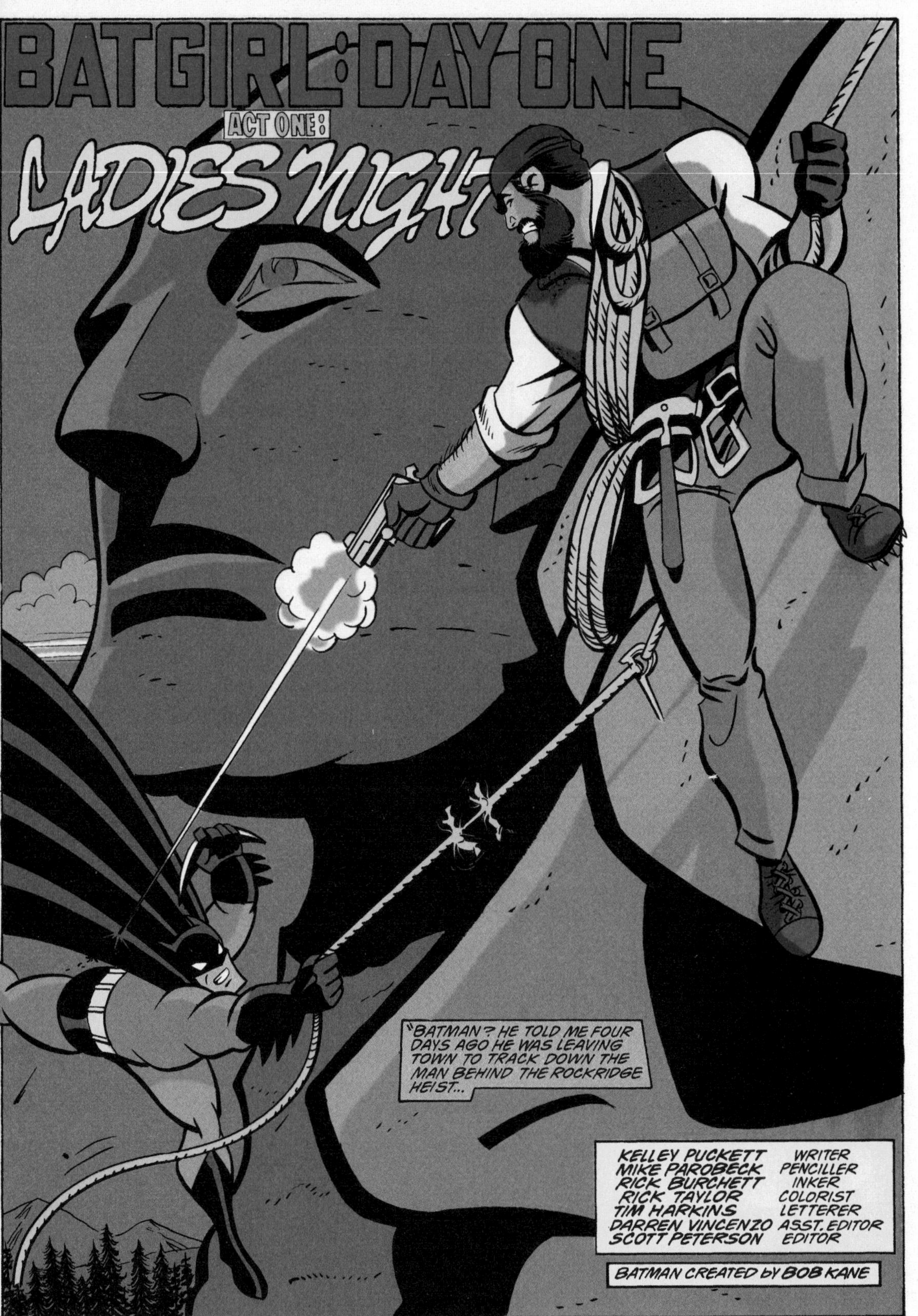
BATGIRL: DAY ONE
ACT ONE:
LADIES NIGHT
"BATMAN? HE TOLD ME FOUR DAYS AGO HE WAS LEAVING TOWN TO TRACK DOWN THE MAN BEHIND THE ROCKRIDGE HEIST...
KELLEY PUCKETT WRITER
MIKE PAROBECK PENCILLER
RICK BURCHETT INKER
RICK TAYLOR COLORIST
TIM HARKINS LETTERER
DARREN VINCENZO ASST. EDITOR
SCOTT PETERSON EDITOR
BATMAN CREATED BY BOB KANE

...AND AS FAR AS I KNOW, HE HASN'T GOTTEN BACK YET. WHY DO YOU ASK?
OH, NO REASON.

THAT'S NOT WHAT YOU'RE WEARING TO CINDY'S PARTY, IS IT?
HER NAME'S SANDY, DAD. AND IT'S A COSTUME PARTY. I HAVEN'T PUT MINE ON YET.

DAD? DID YOU EVER WONDER WHAT IT'S LIKE... TO BE BATMAN?
WHAT DO YOU MEAN?

YOU KNOW, LEAPING FROM ROOFTOPS... CHASING CRIMINALS... DODGING GUNFIRE... IT JUST SOUNDS SO... EXCITING.
2

THERE'S SOMETHING YOU HAVE TO UNDERSTAND, BARBARA. EVERY NIGHT A LOT OF MEN WITH A LOT OF GUNS TRY TO KILL HIM. EVERY NIGHT.

ALL IT TAKES IS ONE MISTAKE... ONE LUCKY SHOT... AND IT'S OVER.
I ADMIRE BATMAN FOR WHAT HE DOES. BUT I DON'T ENVY HIM. NOBODY SHOULD.

WELL, ENOUGH LECTURING. YOU HAVE FUN AT THE PARTY TONIGHT.
THANKS, DAD.

GOOD THING I DIDN'T SHOW HIM THE COSTUME...
3

Moulton Towers
A COSTUME PARTY! IT'S TOO PERFECT! WE WALK IN, GRAB CINDY--
SANDY. SANDY VANOCOUER.
RIGHT. GRAB HER, WALTZ OUT, AND COLLECT OUR TEN MILLION DOLLAR RANSOM. YOU SURE HE CAN PAY IT?
HER FATHER? OH, YES. VANOCOUER CORPORATION'S WHOLESALE DESTRUCTION OF OLD-GROWTH FORESTS HAS MADE HIM RICH.
RICH OFF THE BLOOD OF SLAUGHTERED TREES!
YOU OKAY?
I'M FINE. LET'S GO.
CATSEYE SECURITY CO.
4

WHO ARE YOU SUPPOSED TO BE?
JUDY

SANDY? I THINK SHE WENT THROUGH THERE!
THANKS!

5

NOBODY ALLOWED BACK HERE. GET BACK TO THE PARTY.

CATSEYE

CATSEYE SECURITY CO.

OKAY. GEEZ.

HEY! YOU GIRLS AIN'T SUPPOSED TA BE HERE!

HERE COMES THE PITCH... SHE SWINGS...

6

... AND... IT'S OUTTA HERE!
CATSEYE SECURITY CO.
KRAKKKK
CATS SEC
WHO'RE YOU? BATMAN'S SQUEEZE?
WHAT? NO!
LOUISVILLE SLUGGER
GEE, THAT'S TOO BAD. YOU COULDA GIVEN HIM THIS MESSAGE FROM ME...
7

# ACT 2 : IF THE SUIT FITS!

HEY!

WHOOOOOOOOOOSH

GIMME THAT!

LEGGO! IT'S MINE!

THUNK

8

OWW!
I DON'T THINK
I DID THAT RIGHT...
HARLEY!
THUD
OUT OF
THE WAY!
HARLEY!
ARE YOU ALL
RIGHT?
SUUURE. I'M JUST
GONNA LIE HERE
FOR A WHILE...
THAT'S THE
SPIRIT.
9

AS FOR YOU...
YOU SHOOT ME, AND I'LL DROP IT!
YOU WOULD TAKE THE LIFE OF AN INNOCENT PLANT? WHAT KIND OF MONSTER ARE YOU?!
YOU WANT IT? CATCH!
KRASH
10

MURDERER!
THUNK

SLAM
THUNK

ARE YOU OKAY?

WHO ARE YOU?
I'M... UHH... I'M BATGIRL. BATMAN COULDN'T MAKE IT.
11

SLAM
COME ON!
I CAN'T BELIEVE WE MADE IT!
WE HAVEN'T MADE IT YET.
YEAH, BUT YOU WERE AMAZING BACK THERE!
YOU THINK SO?
ARE YOU KIDDING? YOU JUST BEAT UP HARLEY QUINN AND POISON IVY!
I GUESS I DID, DIDN'T I? YOU KNOW, THIS ISN'T AS TOUGH AS I THOUGHT IT'D BE!
12

HEY, BAT-CHICK!

PAYBACK.

BLAM

13

HMF. MISSED. WELL, IF AT FIRST YOU DON'T SUCCEED...

WAP

THANK GOD! SHE TRIED TO KILL ME!

WAP
UNH
14

WELL, WELL...
...LOOK WHAT THE CAT'S DRAGGED IN.
CATWOMAN!
15

ACT 3: OUT OF THE FRYING PAN!
SO, TRYING TO HORN IN ON OUR ACTION, EH?
HARDLY.
YOU SEE, ON DISPLAY IN THE ROOM ABOVE US IS THE SURH DIAMOND. IT'S THE FIRST TIME THE EMIR OF O'TAR HAS LET IT OUT OF THE COUNTRY.
WHRRR
THE SECURITY ON THAT FLOOR IS TOP-NOTCH. THE SECURITY ON THIS FLOOR ISN'T. ESPECIALLY ONCE I REPLACED THE REAL SECURITY GUARDS WITH MY OWN.
BUT COMMISSIONER GORDON PERSONALLY GUARANTEED THE SAFETY OF THAT DIAMOND!
YES, I KNOW. A LITTLE SURE OF HIMSELF, DON'T YOU THINK?

WE BROKE THROUGH, CATWOMAN! WE'RE IN!
DON'T MOVE. DON'T EVEN BREATHE.
CIAO, GIRLS. KISS, KISS!
17

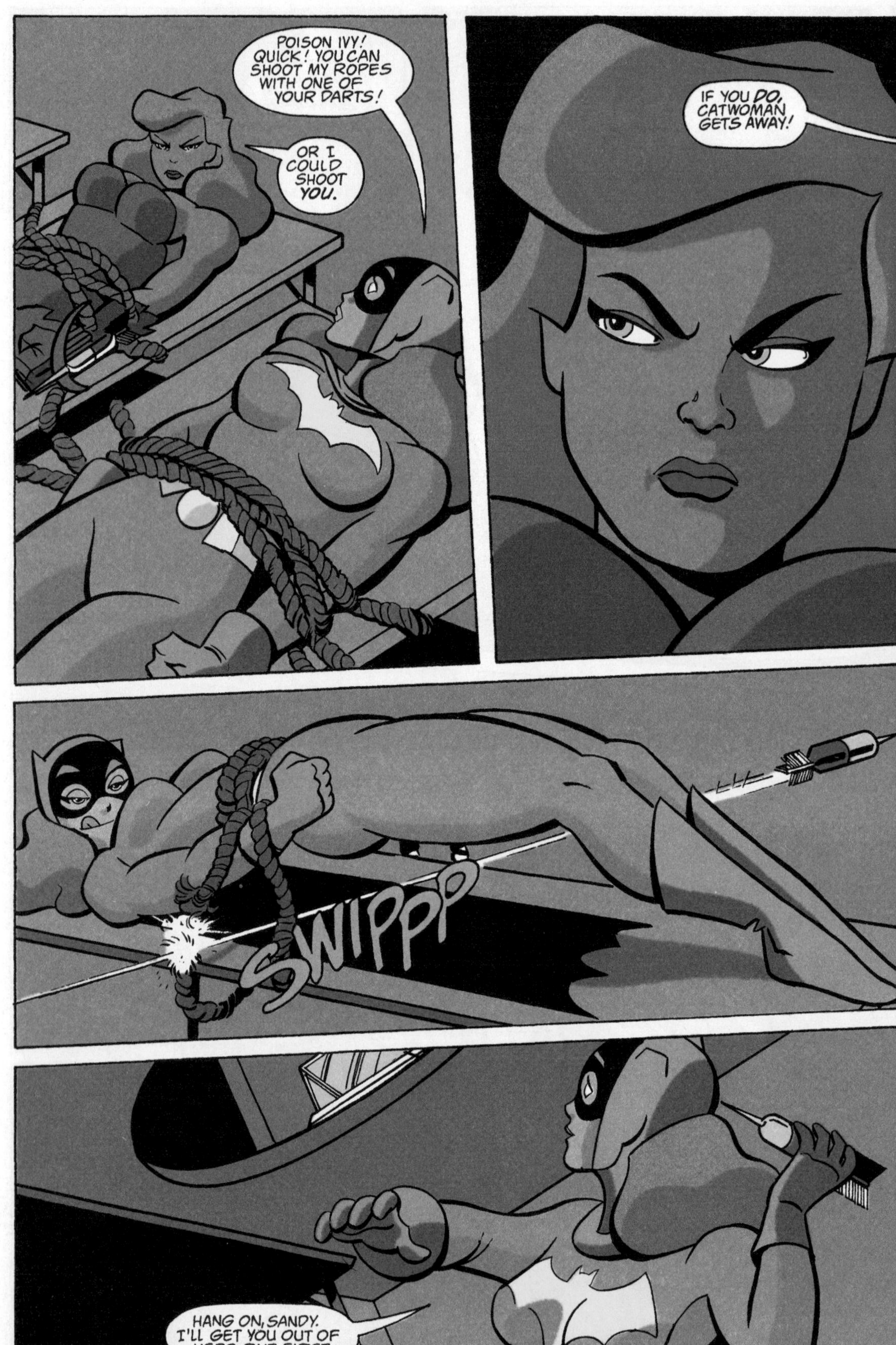
POISON IVY! QUICK! YOU CAN SHOOT MY ROPES WITH ONE OF YOUR DARTS!
OR I COULD SHOOT *YOU*.
IF YOU *DO*, CATWOMAN GETS AWAY!
SWIPPP
HANG ON, SANDY. I'LL GET YOU OUT OF HERE. BUT FIRST...

KRASH
RING
RING RING
RING
RING
RING
SO, ARE YOU... UH... DOING ANYTHING SPECIAL AFTER THE ROBBERY?
THE ALARM?! QUICK! GET IN THE ELEVATOR!
CHANGE OF PLANS. YOU BOYS DISTRACT THE COPS DOWNSTAIRS WHILE I MAKE OFF WITH THE DIAMOND, OKAY?
BUT... BUT THAT'S NOT FAIR. WE'LL ALL GET ARRESTED!
TELL YOU WHAT. NEXT TIME, I'LL HOLD OFF THE COPS AND YOU GUYS CAN GET AWAY.
RING RING RING RING RING
19

EXIT
MUST BE SOMETHING ABOUT THAT Y CHROMOSOME...

WHA--?

YOU?!
DON'T COME ANY CLOSER, CATWOMAN.

SNIK

SNIK

SNIK

SNIK
YOU'RE OUT OF YOUR LEAGUE, LITTLE GIRL. THIS ISN'T FUN AND GAMES.
20

I KNOW THAT NOW. BUT I CAN'T LET YOU TAKE THE DIAMOND.
NO!

GRRRR
I THINK I HEAR THE POLICE COMING...
YOU'LL REGRET THIS. I NEVER FORGET A *BAT*.

THAT WAS *CLOSE*.
21

DAD!
SO YOU'RE NOT REALLY A TRAMP..
BARBARA! ARE YOU ALL RIGHT?
I'M FINE, DAD. I WASN'T ANYWHERE NEAR THE ACTION. SPENT THE WHOLE TIME EATING MUNCHIES.
WHAT HAPPENED TO YOUR COSTUME?
OH, THAT. I THREW IT AWAY. TURNS OUT IT DIDN'T FIT.
THE END

WIN ORIGINAL BATMAN ADVENTURES ART!
DETAILS INSIDE!
APPROVED BY THE COMICS CODE AUTHORITY
US $1.25
CAN $1.60
UK 70p
FOX KIDS NETWORK
THE BATMAN ADVENTURES
PUCKETT
PAROBECK
BURCHETT

LAST TANGO IN PARIS
"... WALKED INTO HEADQUARTERS AND STARTED THROWING PUNCHES, BEGGING TO BE PUT IN JAIL. I INTERROGATED HIM MYSELF, BUT DIDN'T GET A WORD OUT OF HIM."
"DID YOU GET AN ADDRESS?"
KELLEY PUCKETT WRITER
MIKE PAROBECK PENCILLER
RICK BURCHETT INKER
RICK TAYLOR COLORIST
TIM HARKINS LETTERER
DARREN VINCENZO ASS'T ED.
SCOTT PETERSON EDITOR
ACT 1: OLD FLAME
BATMAN CREATED BY BOB KANE

"SURE. 545 MOSSWOOD. APARTMENT NUMBER 28."
2

3

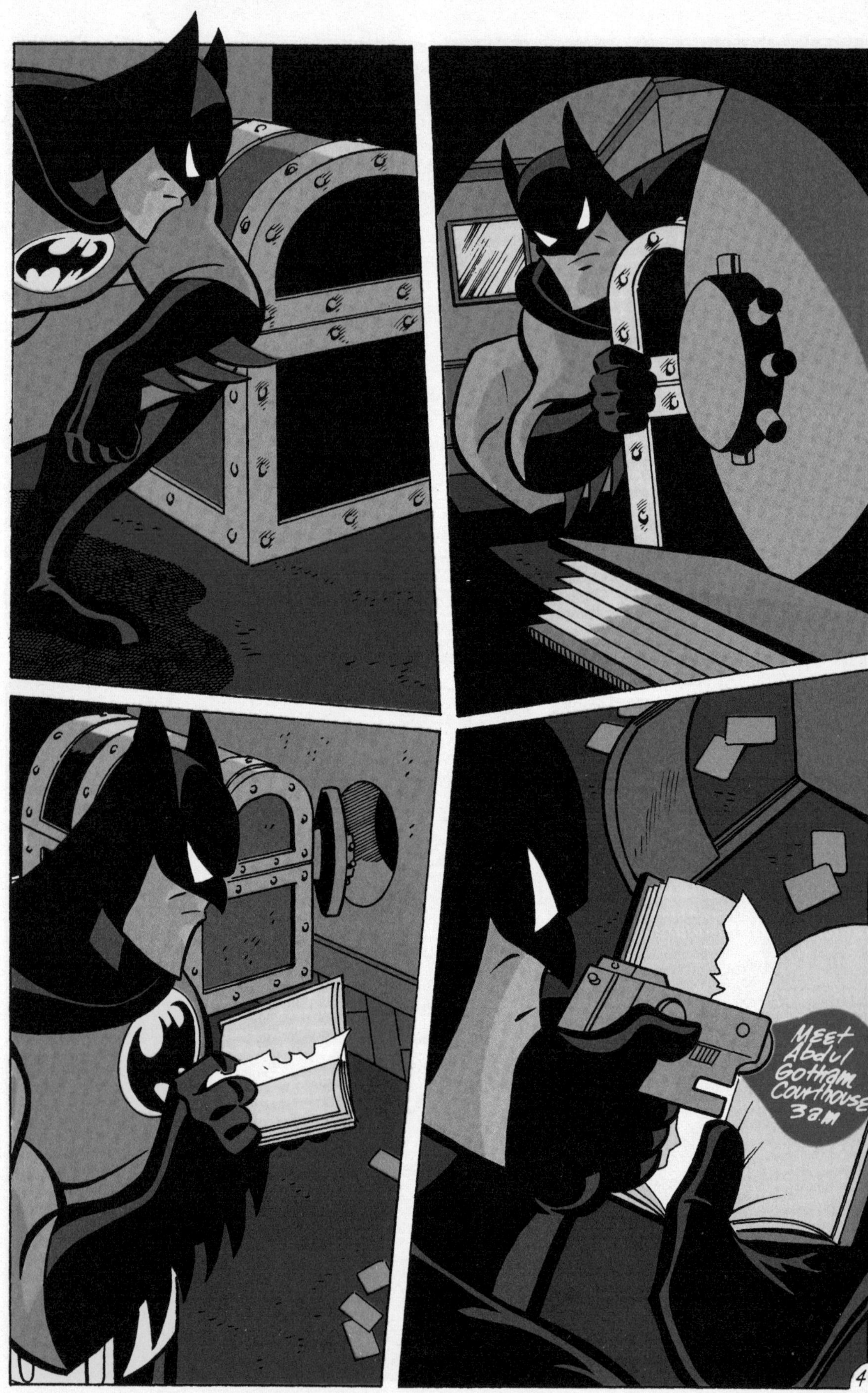
MEET
Abdul
Gotham
Courthouse
3 a.m
4

I SWEAR TO YOU THAT'S ALL I KNOW. PLEASE, MISTRESS... HAVE MERCY...
I CAME FOR INFORMATION, ABDUL. VENGEANCE WILL COME FOR YOU LATER. RELEASE HIM.

BUT MISTRESS! YOUR FATHER--
-- WILL BE CROSS WITH ME WHEN HE LEARNS I LET HIM LIVE. I KNOW.
GOOD DECISION.

WHY HELLO, DETECTIVE.
HELLO, TALIA.
INFIDEL!

NONE MAY TOUCH THE DAUGHTER OF RA'S AL GHUL!
STOP, YOU IDIOT!
5

CHOK
KRAK
6

I APOLOGIZE. THEY ARE FOOLS, BUT THEY SERVE MY FATHER WELL.
WHY DID YOU COME TO GOTHAM, TALIA?
A TRUSTED EMPLOYEE OF MY FATHER'S STOLE A STATUE OF GREAT VALUE FROM HIM. THE THIEF HAD TWO ACCOMPLICES-- THE MAN YOU JUST SAW...
...AND THE ONE AT 545 MOSSWOOD.
YES. I LEAVE GOTHAM TONIGHT TO CONTINUE MY SEARCH. I KNOW YOU WILL FOLLOW ME, DETECTIVE. I SUGGEST WE TRAVEL TOGETHER.
WHY?
WHY NOT?
WHERE IS THIS "THIEF" NOW?
7

# ACT 2: PARIS IS BURNING!

TALIA? HOW DID YOU GET IN HERE?
A YOUNG WOMAN ASKING FOR THE ROOM KEY OF INTERNATIONAL PLAYBOY BRUCE WAYNE? THIS *IS* PARIS.
AND IT'S FAR TOO BEAUTIFUL A DAY TO SLEEP THROUGH. I'LL EXPECT YOU IN THE LOBBY IN TEN MINUTES. AND JUST SO YOU KNOW...
... *MOST* OF THE PLACES WE'LL BE VISITING REQUIRE *CLOTHES*.
MAP OF PARIS
9

Blue Heaven Café

I WASN'T SURE YOU'D AGREE TO SPEND THE DAY WITH ME. I'M GLAD YOU DID.
SO AM I.

WE SHOULD GO. IT'LL BE DARK SOON.

MAGNIFICATION 109
METERS 121
THAT'S HASSAN. THE THIEF WHO BETRAYED MY FATHER.
SPX FACTOR 52
ABDUL SAID HASSAN WOULD MEET HERE WITH A MAN NAMED PIERRE LASCAUX. LASCAUX IS AN OLD ENEMY OF MY FATHER'S AND IS WILLING TO RISK BUYING THE STATUE.
NO OTHER CARS- HASSAN ARRIVED FIRST. STAY HERE.
KNOCK
KNOCK
12

QUI EST LA?! WHO'S THERE?!
SMASH
I WANT THE STATUE.
IT'S IN THERE! IN THERE!
I WOULD SUGGEST THAT YOU STAY VERY STILL...
13

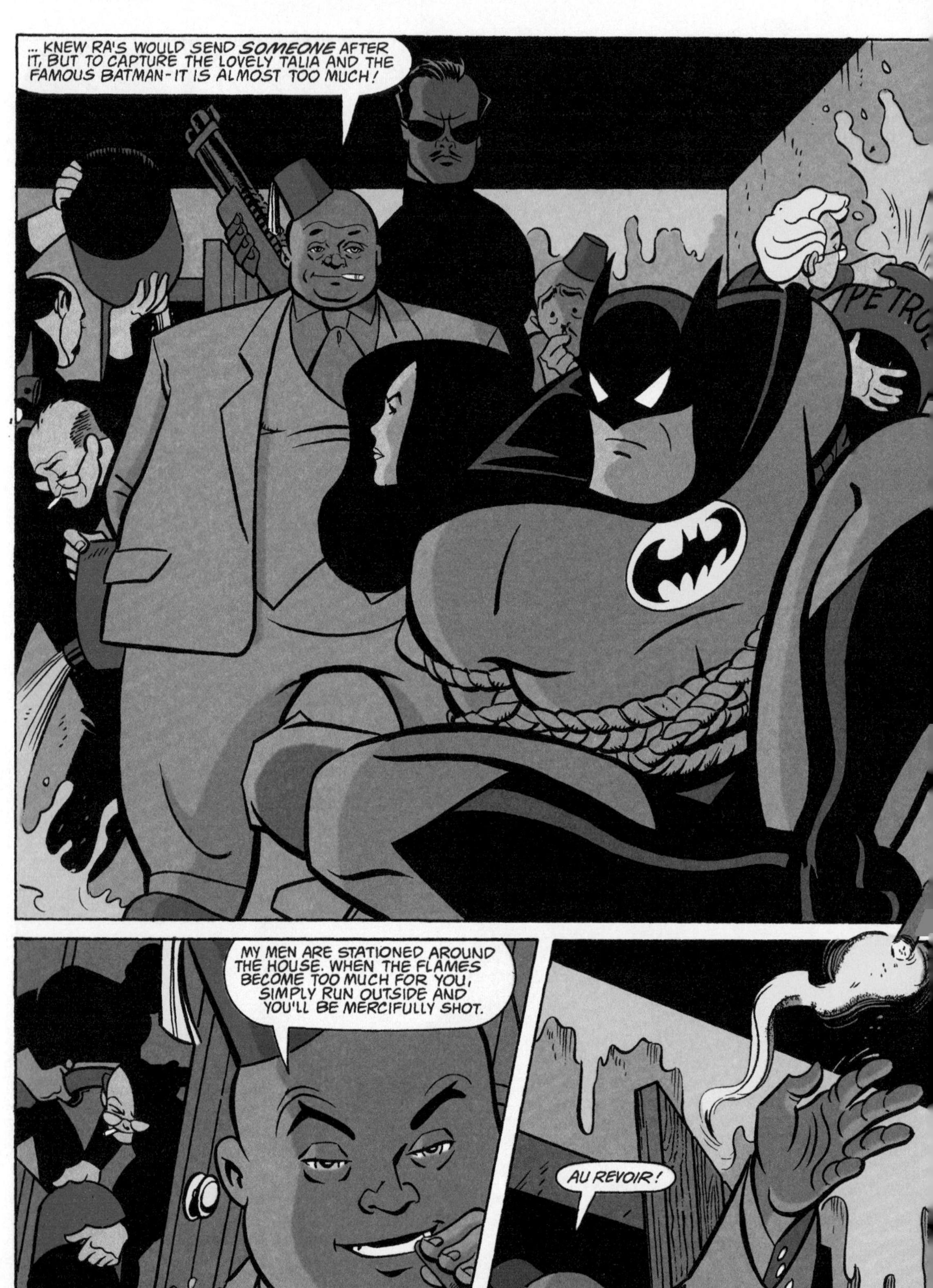

... KNEW RA'S WOULD SEND *SOMEONE* AFTER IT, BUT TO CAPTURE THE LOVELY TALIA AND THE FAMOUS BATMAN - IT IS ALMOST TOO MUCH!
MY MEN ARE STATIONED AROUND THE HOUSE. WHEN THE FLAMES BECOME TOO MUCH FOR YOU, SIMPLY RUN OUTSIDE AND YOU'LL BE MERCIFULLY SHOT.
AU REVOIR!

# ACT 3: WHERE THERE'S SMOKE!

YOU KNOW WHAT TO DO?

YES. BUT WHAT YOU ARE DOING IS SO DANGEROUS... I MUST KNOW SOMETHING FIRST.

WHEN YOU TURNED DOWN MY FATHER'S OFFER TO MARRY ME AND TAKE HIS PLACE... WAS IT *ONLY* BECAUSE YOU HATE MY FATHER'S WORK? OR DID YOU... NOT FIND ME...

15

BE CAREFUL.

16

17

BLAM
BLAM

GO! QUICKLY! KILL THE BATMAN!

I COULD HAVE JUST *SHOT* HIM, BUT *NO!* I MUST LOCK HIM IN A BURNING BUILDING!

*WHY?!* WHY MUST I HAVE SO MUCH *STYLE?*

WHERE IS HE?

18

VRROOOOOM
BLAM
PTOW!
19

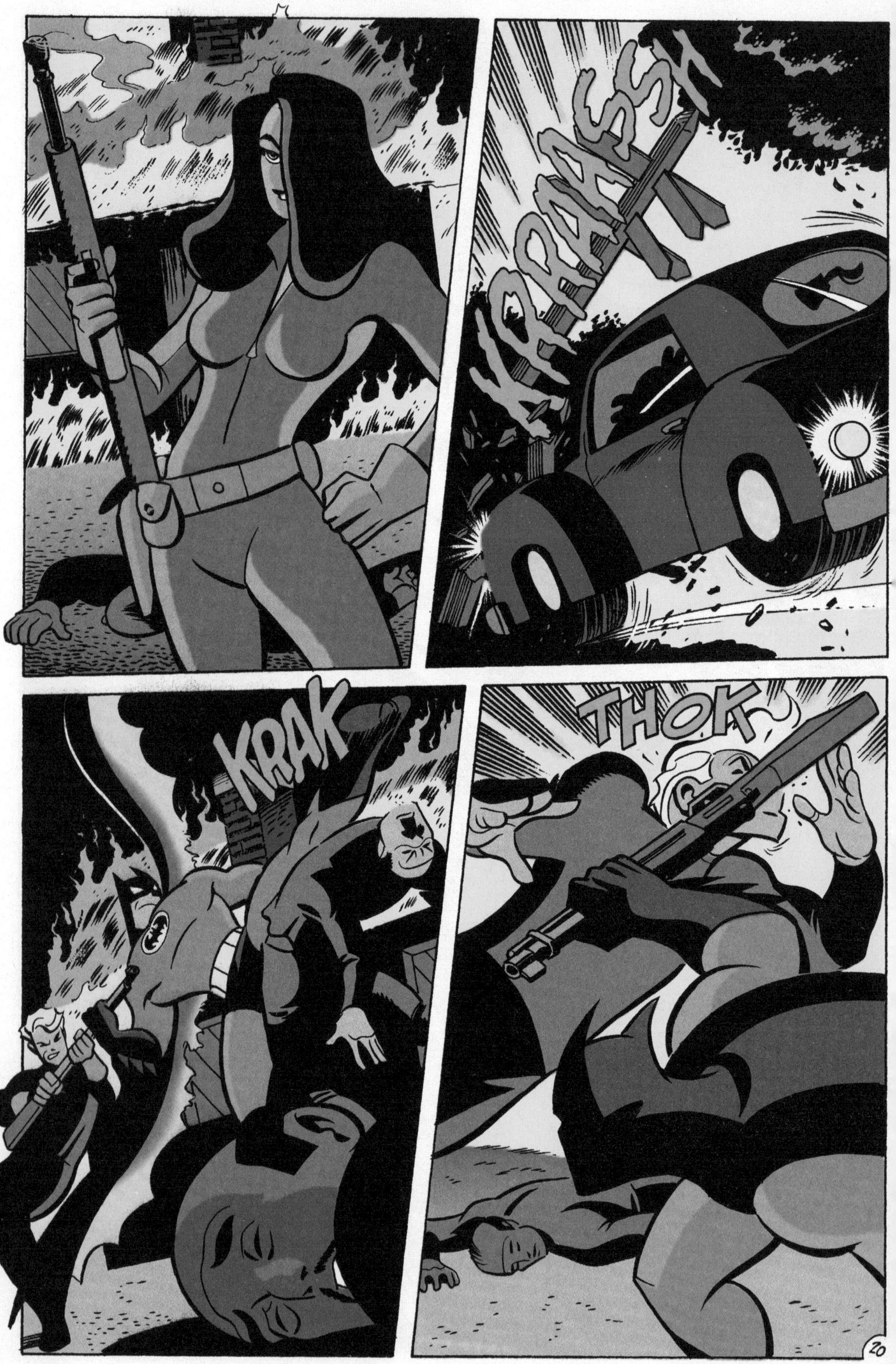

KRRASSH

KRAK

THOK

20

I HAVE IT! THE STATUE!
GOOD. NOW TELL ME WHAT'S INSIDE IT.

HOW DID YOU--
MICROFILM. IT CONTAINS INFORMATION EXTREMELY DAMAGING TO MY FATHER'S OPERATIONS. LASCAUX MASTERMINDED THE THEFT.

I SHOULD HAVE TOLD YOU EARLIER, BUT...
BUT IF YOU TOLD ME YOU WOULDN'T HAVE HAD A *PATSY*.

NO! IF I'D TOLD YOU...
...WE WOULDN'T HAVE HAD PARIS.
21

THE END

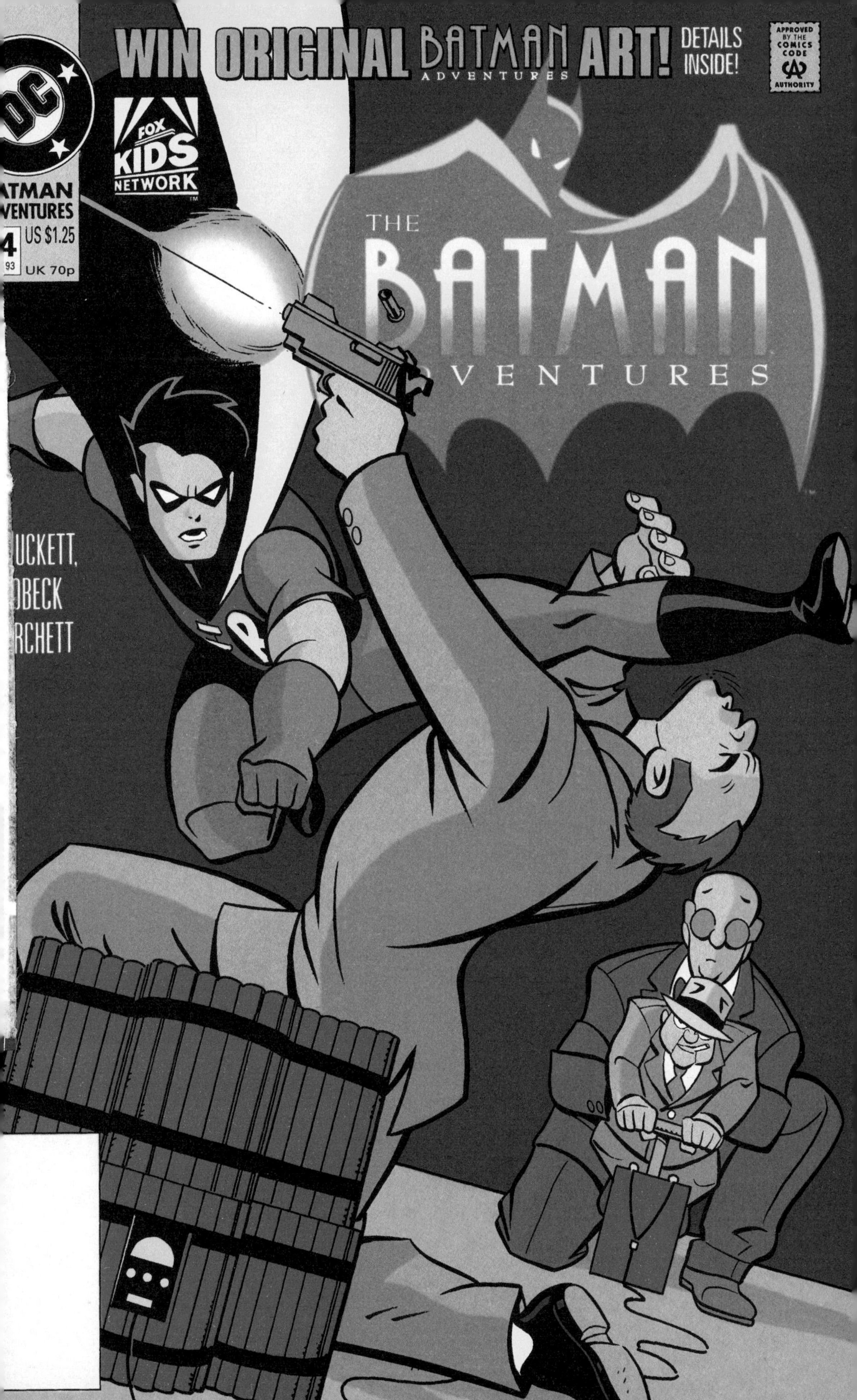
WIN ORIGINAL BATMAN ADVENTURES ART! DETAILS INSIDE!
APPROVED BY THE COMICS CODE AUTHORITY
DC
FOX KIDS NETWORK
BATMAN ADVENTURES
4 US $1.25
UK 70p
THE BATMAN ADVENTURES
UCKETT,
OBECK
RCHETT

NO! WHAT YOU DON'T UNDERSTAND IS THAT I'M TRYING TO RUN A PROTECTION RACKET HERE!
NOW IF YOU DON'T GOT THE MONEY--
DING DING
WHAT WAS THAT?!

KRAK
KELLEY PUCKETT WRITER MIKE PAROGECK PENCILLER
RICK GURCHETT INKER RICK TAYLOR COLORIST
TIM HARKINS LETTERER DARREN VINCENZO ASS'T ED.
SCOTT PETERSON EDITOR
GATMAN CREATED
GY GOG KANE

PUBLIC ENEMY
ACT 1: BREAKOUT!

CHOK

BONK

CALL THE POLICE. THEY'LL TAKE CARE OF THESE GUYS FOR YOU.
ROBIN BOY WONDER! YOU SAVE MY STORE! HEY, YOU HUNGRY? I GOT SOME NICE CAPICOLLA...

... SANDWICHES AND TEA BEFORE YOU RETIRE ?
THANKS, ALFRED, BUT I... UH... PICKED UP SOMETHING ON THE WAY HOME.

MASTER BRUCE PHONED EARLIER. HE WISHED TO THANK YOU AGAIN FOR "FILLING IN" ON SUCH SHORT NOTICE.
HEY, NO PROBLEM. I'D ALMOST FORGOTTEN HOW MUCH I ENJOY THIS STUFF.

I MEAN, COLLEGE IS FUN AND ALL, BUT WHAT I DO AS ROBIN IS SO MUCH MORE... IMPORTANT, YOU KNOW ?
INDEED.

IN FACT, I THINK I'LL STAY UP AND LOOK OVER SOME OF BRUCE'S NEW FILES. DON'T WAIT UP FOR ME.
AS YOU WISH.
5

ARKHAM ASYLUM
SKKRAAKK
SCARFACE
FREE!! I'M FREE!!!
DEY AIN'T GUILT THE CAGE DAT CAN HOLD SCARFACE! HA HA HA HA HA--

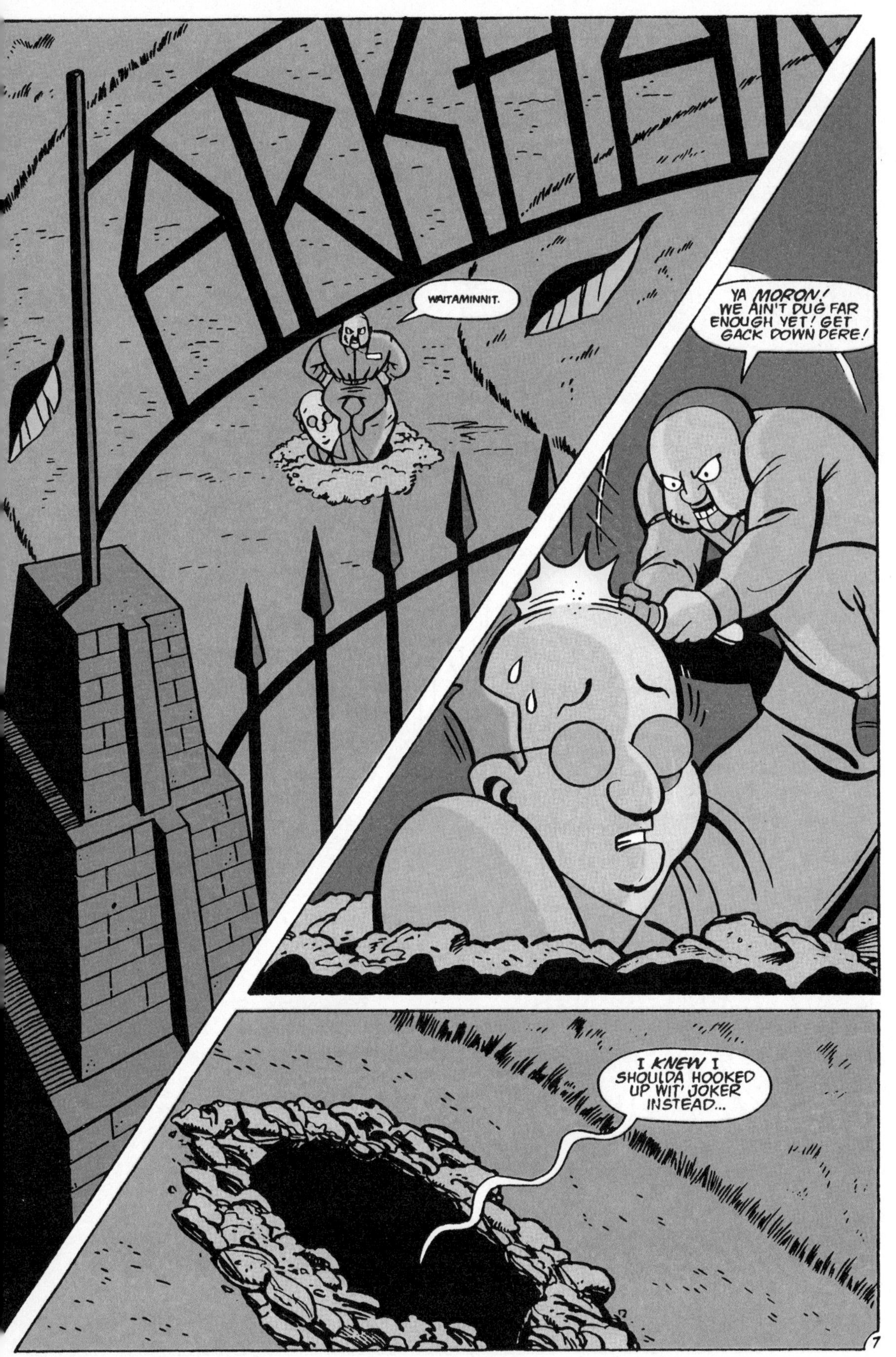
WAITAMINNIT.
YA MORON! WE AIN'T DUG FAR ENOUGH YET! GET GACK DOWN DERE!
I KNEW I SHOULDA HOOKED UP WIT' JOKER INSTEAD...
7

# ACT 2: THE GRINKS JOG

GOTHAM FIRST

WYDOWN

SECREASE

EVERYGODY HIT DA FLOOR! DIS IS A GANK ROGGERY!

A GANK ROGGERY!!!
BUDDA BUDDA BUDDA BUDDA
HEY, BOSS! DIS LADY PUSHED THE SILENT ALARM BUTTON!
PERFECT! DIS JOG IS GOIN' LIKE CLOCKWORK!
9

I'VE CLEANED YOUR OUTFIT, MASTER DICK.
YOU MAY HAVE TO GET USED TO DOING THAT AGAIN, ALFRED. I'M THINKING OF STAYING.
LIBERTY

AND POSTPONING YOUR RETURN TO THE UNIVERSITY? WE'LL BE MOST HAPPY TO HAVE YOU...
MAD HATTER
NOT POSTPONING, ALFRED. QUITTING. BEING ROBIN FULL-TIME AGAIN.
PROF.

I FINALLY REALIZED THERE'S NO POINT IN FINISHING OUT SCHOOL IF I'M JUST GOING TO RETURN TO BEING ROBIN AFTERWARDS.
I WAS UNAWARE YOU'D MADE THAT DECISION.

WELL, IT'S NOT MUCH OF A DECISION, IS IT? I MEAN, HOW COULD I POSSIBLY LEAVE ALL OF *THIS* BEHIND?

AT THE RISK OF BORING YOU, SIR, I'D LIKE TO RELATE AN EPISODE FROM MY OWN LIFE.
OF COURSE, ALFRED.

I HAD A SIMILAR CHOICE TO MAKE AS A YOUNG MAN- WHETHER TO FOLLOW IN MY FATHER'S FOOTSTEPS AS A MANSERVANT OR PURSUE A CAREER IN THE THEATRE.
TRUST

YOU SEE, ACTING HAD BEEN MY LIFE, AND ALTHOUGH I KNEW EVEN THEN THAT IT WASN'T WHAT I WAS MEANT TO DO, I FOUND IT... *EXTREMELY* DIFFICULT TO LEAVE BEHIND.

PERHAPS YOU'RE MEANT TO BE DICK GRAYSON. PERHAPS ROBIN. BUT YOU WON'T MAKE THE RIGHT DECISION IF YOU'RE UNWILLING TO LET GO OF THE PAST.
ALL UNITS! ALL UNITS! HOSTAGE SITUATION AT GOTHAM FIRST NATIONAL...

GOTHAM FIRST NATIONAL BANK
...AND I WANT THOSE CHOPPERS HOVERING OUT OF SIGHT, BUT WITHIN A MILE OF HERE. GOT IT?
COMMISSIONER GORDON.
GOOD TO SEE YOU, SON.
I'VE GOT UNKNOWN ARMED TERRORISTS IN THERE AND VISUAL CONFIRMATION OF SEVERAL HOSTAGES. THERE'S A LOOKOUT ON THE ROOF AND NO WAY IN FROM BELOW.
ANY DEMANDS YET?
TWO CHOPPERS TO TAKE THEM AND SELECT HOSTAGES TO GOTHAM AIRPORT. FROM THERE A PRIVATE JET-- APPARENTLY THEY HAVE THEIR OWN PILOT.
HOW MUCH TIME CAN YOU GIVE ME?
TWENTY MINUTES. THEN I'M GOING TO HAVE TO GIVE THEM WHAT THEY WANT.

UH, BOSS? HOW COME... WHY DO YA... HOW COME YA SAY "B'S" LIKE THEY'RE "G'S"?

I MEAN, IF YA DON'T WANNA TALK ABOUT IT, DAT'S OKAY...

NAH, I MIGHT AS WELL TELL YA. I GOT INTO A FIGHT IN DA JOINT. GOT MY LIPS RIPPED OFF.

*THAT'S* GOTTA HURT.

OOOH, I *HATE* DAT!

GUT YOU SHOULD SEE DA *OTHER* GUY!

HE AIN'T EVEN GACK ON SOLID *FOOD* YET!

13

I DON'T UNDERSTAND, SCARFACE WHAT'S THE PLAN? WHY DID YOU TELL THE POLICE WE'RE TERRORISTS?
AWRIGHT, I'LL TELL YA THE PLAN. YOU GAVE ME THE IDEA.
WE CLEAR OUT THE VAULT, GRING DA HOSTAGES TO DA ROOF LIKE WE'RE GONNA ESCAPE WIT 'EM, GLOW UP DA ROOF, AND ESCAPE IN DA CONFUSION IN DA AMGULANCE FROM DA UNDERGROUND LOT.
BOOOM
BUT... THAT'S NOT A PLAN! THAT'S A MOVIE I TOLD YOU ABOUT!
RELAX. AS LONG AS NOGODY ELSE SAW IT, WE'RE SITTIN' PRETTY!

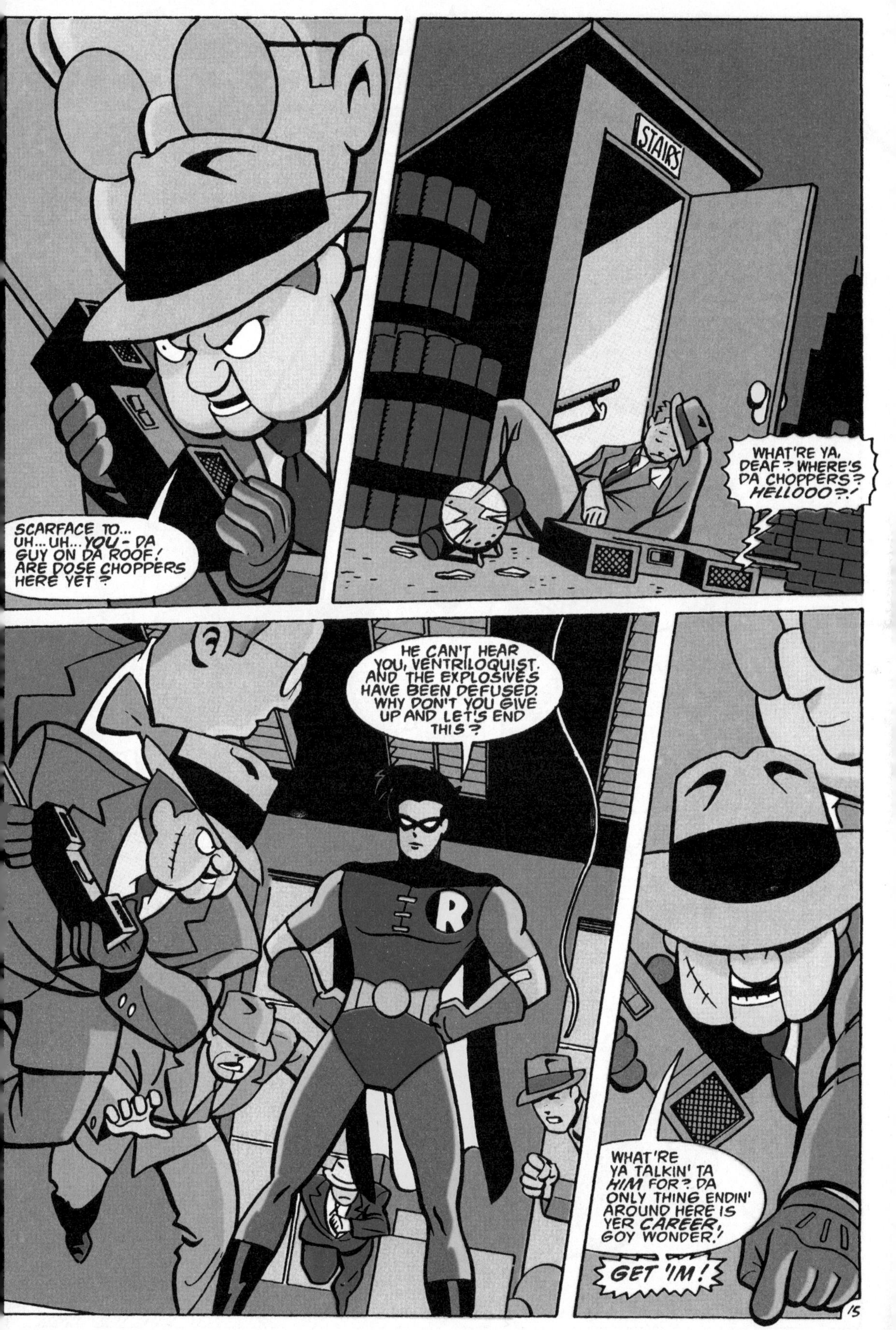

SCARFACE TO... UH... UH... *YOU* - DA GUY ON DA ROOF! ARE DOSE CHOPPERS HERE YET?

STAIRS

WHAT'RE YA, DEAF? WHERE'S DA CHOPPERS? *HELLOOO*?!

HE CAN'T HEAR YOU, VENTRILOQUIST. AND THE EXPLOSIVES HAVE BEEN DEFUSED. WHY DON'T YOU GIVE UP AND LET'S END THIS?

WHAT'RE YA TALKIN' TA *HIM* FOR? DA ONLY THING ENDIN' AROUND HERE IS YER *CAREER*, GOY WONDER!

*GET 'IM!*

15

# ACT 3: THE GIG CLOCK!

WHA-?

OW! OW! OW!

THUD

16

WHAK

CHOK

KRAK
17

GRAVO, ROGIN! NOW I'M GIVIN' YA SIXTY SECONDS TA CLEAR OUT! YA CAN'T DEFUSE DIS ONE!

HOLD YOUR FIRE! GET ME SOME BLANKETS

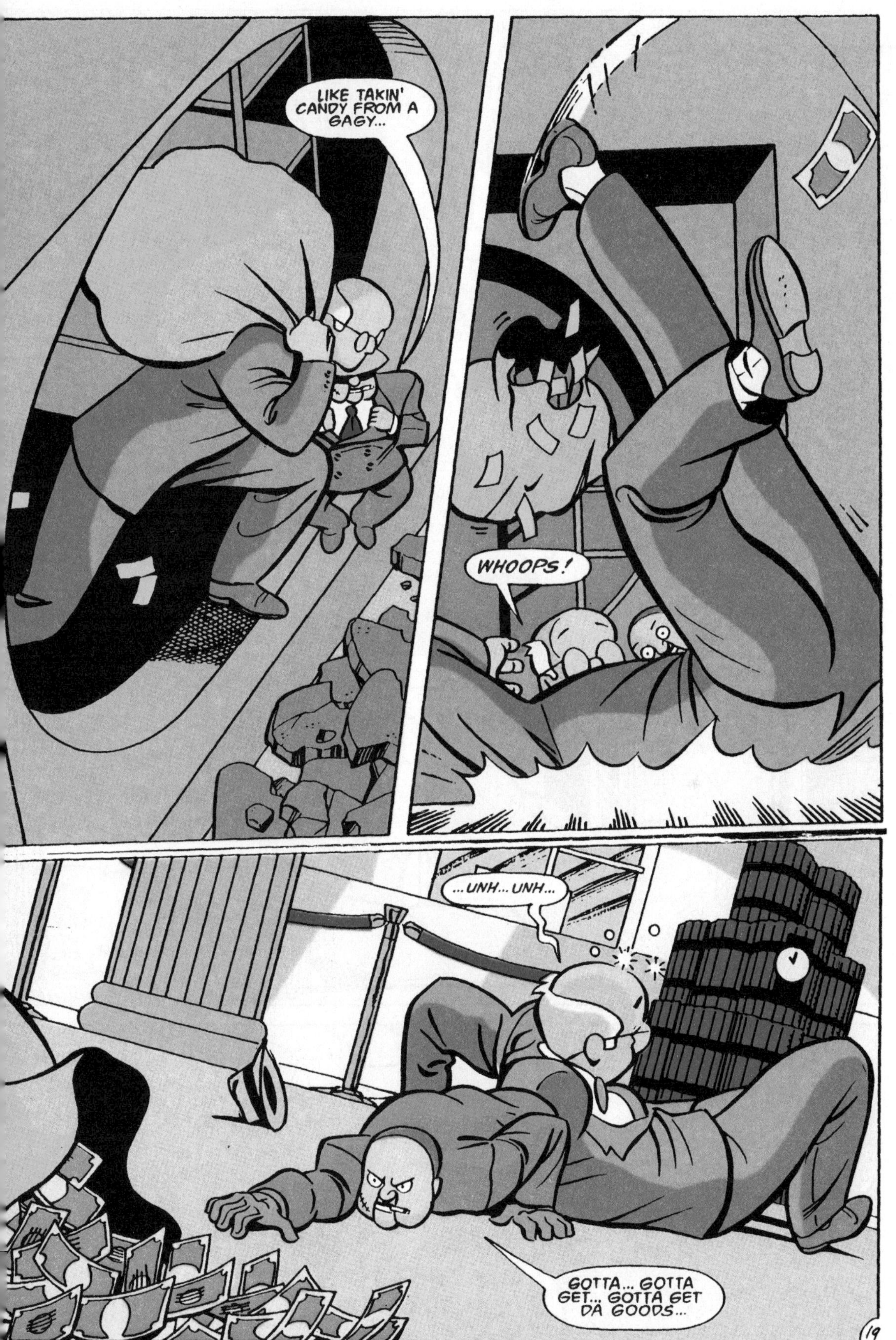
LIKE TAKIN' CANDY FROM A GAGY...
WHOOPS!
...UNH... UNH...
GOTTA... GOTTA GET... GOTTA GET DA GOODS...
19

... WHA? SCARFACE... WHAT'RE YOU DOING? THE DYNAMITE! THERE'S ONLY A FEW SECONDS LEFT!
TICK

... MUSTN'T... GLACK... OUT...
TICK
SCARFACE! PLEASE!

VENTRILOQUIST! LEAVE HIM! LET GO OF HIM!
TICK

I CAN'T!
TICK
20

21

...USEFUL, BUT RA'S RENDERED MOST OF IT OBSOLETE ALREADY.
THAT'S TOO BAD. DID YOU THINK ABOUT--
PARDON MY INTERRUPTION, BUT IT IS HALF PAST.
OH, MAN. YOU'RE RIGHT. I'VE GOT TO HEAD BACK TO SCHOOL.
WELL, THANKS AGAIN. BESIDES THE VENTRILOQUIST, DID ANYTHING ELSE HAPPEN I SHOULD KNOW ABOUT?
NO, THAT'S IT. SEE YA LATER, BRUCE.
DID I MISS SOMETHING HERE?
THE END

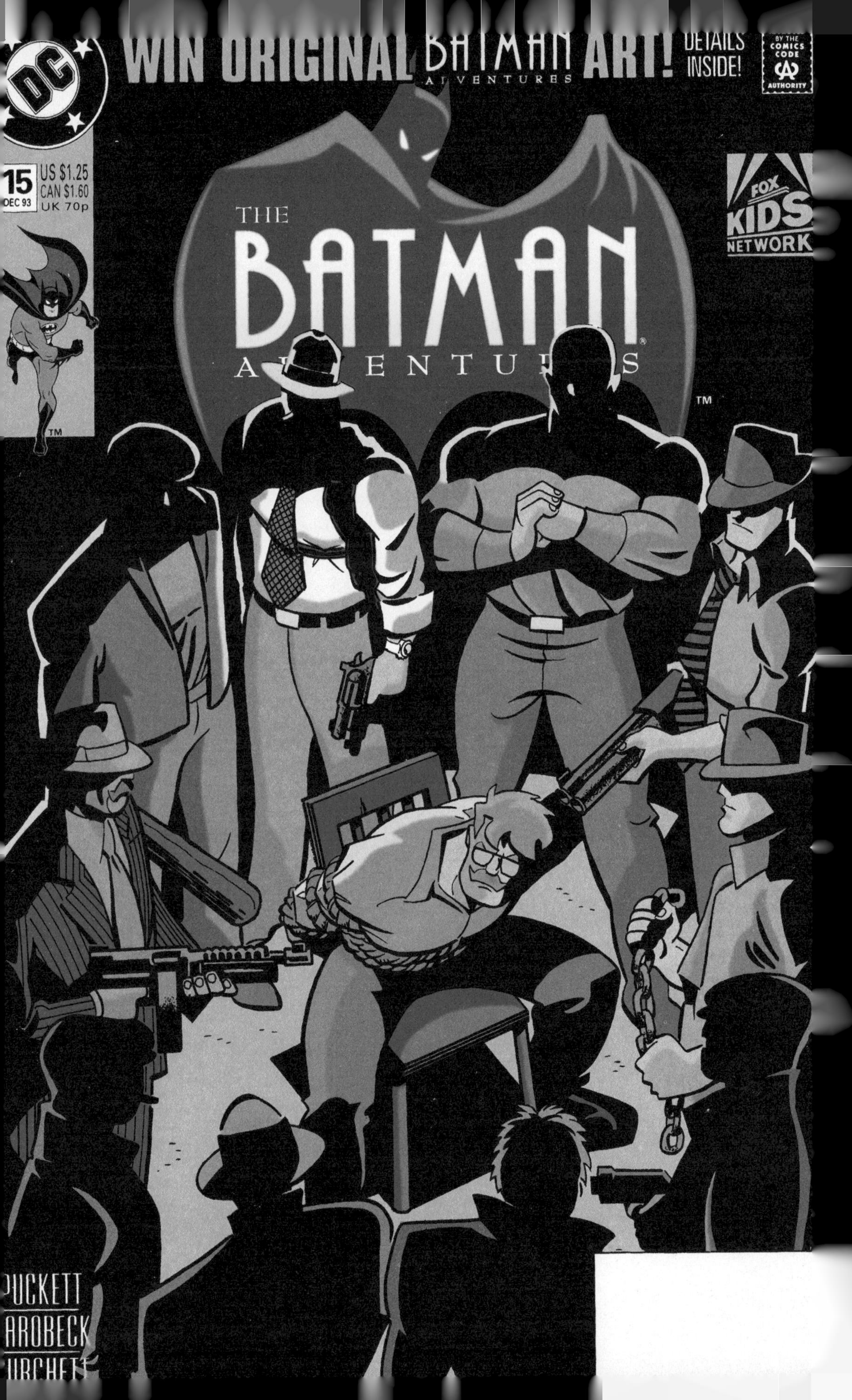

DC
WIN ORIGINAL BATMAN ADVENTURES ART!
DETAILS INSIDE!
BY THE COMICS CODE AUTHORITY
15
DEC 93
US $1.25
CAN $1.60
UK 70p
FOX KIDS NETWORK
THE BATMAN ADVENTURES
TM

BADGE OF HONOR
...IMAGINE MISTER THORNE'S SURPRISE WHEN HE FOUND OUT HIS GOOD FRIEND "JOE BRODY" WAS REALLY A COP!
His cover's blown. Thorne's going to kill him.
GOTHAM CITY
POLI
ACT ONE: OFFICER DOWN!
KELLEY PUCKETT WRITER
MIKE PAROBECK PENCILLER
RICK BURCHETT INKER
RICK TAYLOR COLORIST
TIM HARKINS LETTERER
DARREN VINCENZO ASS'T. ED.
SCOTT PETERSON EDITOR
BATMAN CREATED BY BOB KANE

NOW, MISTER THORNE'S A CIVILIZED MAN -- IF YOU TURN OVER ALL THE INFO THE COP FOUND OUT WITHIN TWENTY-FOUR HOURS, YOU GET HIM BACK IN ONE PIECE.
Miller wouldn't talk. Smart.

BUT IF YOU TRY ANYTHING *FUNNY*,
Thorne'll keep him alive until he's got the information, but no longer. Not after Miller got that close to him. I've got to stall for time. But first...

I DON'T MAKE DEALS WITH TWO-BIT GOONS LIKE YOU.
I really shouldn't do this. I need for Thorne to think I'll play along.

HEY! YOU WATCH YER MOUTH!
GET THAT THING OUT OF MY FACE.
I need to sound desperate. Eager to please.

But my job means nothing if thugs like this can wave guns at a cop and get away with it.
I'LL POINT IT WHEREVER I --
KRAK
3

DROP 'EM. RIGHT NOW.

...WHICH IS WHY I CAN'T BRING THE FORCE IN ON THIS.

DON'T WORRY, JIM. I'LL FIND HIM.

NO. *I* WILL.

EITHER SOMEBODY IN THE DEPARTMENT BLEW HIS COVER OR HE DID IT HIMSELF. EITHER WAY, *I'M* RESPONSIBLE.

MILLER WAS IN DEEP. HE REALLY BURNED THORNE. WHEN IT COMES TIME TO PULL THE TRIGGER, THORNE WILL DO IT HIMSELF.
I WANT YOU TO SHADOW HIM.

THAT WAY IF I DON'T MAKE IT, YOU'LL STILL BE ABLE TO STOP THORNE IN TIME.
THOSE HOODS CAME BY MY APARTMENT AT TWO THIRTY...

...AND IT'S ALMOST FOUR THIRTY NOW. WE'VE GOT TWENTY-TWO HOURS.
TRY TO SLEEP, JIM. AND BE CAREFUL OUT THERE.

These files Miller got us are excellent police work. Perceptive. Observant. Detailed.
DET. ANTON MILLER

Tony Wiesel. My best shot at finding out where they're keeping him.
E: Tony Wiesel
K: Lieutenant. A
mber of Thorne's
er circle (see
low)
SPONSIBILITIES:
Mostly numbers-run-
ing and other low-
profile activities,
Wiesel also runs an
underground nightclub
(2nd Avenue and
Fifth Street).
EVALUATION: Wiesel
has made himself use-
ful to Thorne by ratting
out disloyal members of the organization, but
his incompetence and cowardice weigh heavily
against him. Thorne is openly contemptuous
of him (calling him "weasel" in front of the
others), and there are rumors of Wiesel's
being "edged out" of the inner circle in the
near future. This, combined with Wiesel's
extreme fear of imprisonment (see page fo
make him an ideal candidate for turning
state's evidence in the future. Lament re-

Sounds made to order, but if Wiesel doesn't come through, I don't know what I'll--

I'll think of something else. Find another way.
I'm not going to lose another good cop.
7

ACT TWO: COP KILLER!
Wiesel's club. This has to go smoothly.
SORRY, POPS. I THINK YOU GOT THE WRONG PLACE.
OPEN THE DOOR. TELL WEASEL I WANT TO TALK.
GOTHAM CITY
POLICE
Nice place.
Bilge BEER
KNOCK
KNOCK KNOCK

KNOCK
KNOCK KNOCK
...REALLY HIM! HE SHOWED ME HIS BADGE!
OKAY. J-JUST STAY CALM!
PRIVATE
DON'T MOVE.
WHY, YA--
PRIVAT
KRAK
9

DON'T TRY IT.

EVERYBODY OUT. I WANT TO TALK TO WEASEL IN PRIVATE.

I-IT'S WIE*SEL*. THE ACCENT'S ON THE S-SECOND SYL--
YOU'VE GOT TEN SECONDS TO TELL ME WHERE THEY'RE HOLDING THE UNDERCOVER OFFICER. IF YOU DON'T, I'LL BUST YOU FOR SELLING LIQUOR WITHOUT A LICENSE.

WHAT? TH-THAT'S *KID* STUFF!
OH, I KNOW. YOU'LL ONLY BE IN JAIL A FEW WEEKS, *TOPS*. PIECE OF CAKE FOR A TOUGH GUY LIKE YOU...

Warehouse on the South Side. Good hideout.
Five men. All sitting, guns visible. This is as good a chance as I'll get.

ON YOUR FEET! HANDS UP!

DON'T EVEN THINK ABOUT MOVING.
OR WHAT? YOU CAN'T DROP US ALL, GORDON.

YOU'RE RIGHT. THIS BEING A REVOLVER AND CONSIDERING MY ADVANCED AGE, I'D BET I CAN ONLY TAKE OUT THE FIRST THREE OF YOU THAT MOVE.
WHO'S IT GOING TO BE?
11

They're too relaxed. They should be squirming, debating whether to take their chances with me or with Thorne.
I'm missing something.
That chair! There's six of them!
But where--
WHAM
...

Wha--?
Hit from behind. Must've blacked out.

They should've put a gun on me.
KRAK

Twenty years ago I could've fought my way out of here.
THAP
13

CHOK
It's no good. One more shot like that--
WHAK
THOK
WH
AM

...SHOULD HAVE LET ME KNOW SOONER. I'M ALWAYS INTERESTED IN DOING BUSINESS WITH MY FRIENDS IN DETROIT.
THE O'LEARY BROTHERS ARE INTERESTED AS WELL, MISTER THORNE, BUT THEY'RE ...CONCERNED.

WORD IS YOU CAN'T HANDLE BATMAN OR THE COPS.
LIES PERPETRATED BY MY ENEMIES. THE SITUATION IS UNDER CONTROL--
RING RING

THIS BETTER BE GOOD.
GORDON TRIED FOR THE COP. WE GOT HIM.
EXCELLENT. BRING THEM IN.

STAY FOR A WHILE LONGER, MY FRIEND. I'LL SHOW YOU SOMETHING THAT'LL PUT ALL YOUR FEARS TO REST.
15

# ACT THREE: CODE DEAD!

REMEMBER! SHOOT ANYTHING THAT MOVES!

MY FAULT, SIR. I'D BEEN TOLD TO ROUGH UP ONE OF THE NUMBER-RUNNERS. JUST A KID. I LET HIM GO...
...AND HE TURNED YOU IN. TYPICAL COP.

DON'T LOOK SO SMUG, THORNE. MILLER WAS ALREADY ABOVE SUSPICION. YOU GOT LUCKY.
YOU WANT TO CALL IT THAT? FINE. LADY LUCK SMILED AT ME...

...BUT SHE JUST RAN OUT ON YOU.
Try to kick the gun. Only chance...
17

unh
It's him.
THUD
I should have known.
THUNK

AAAAHHH!

Thorne's gun.
SMASH

IT'S BATMAN! GET HIM!

This is it.
19

BLAM
BUDDA
DROP THE GUN, GORDON! DROP IT OR I SHOOT THE COP. YOUR CHOICE.
WRONG, THORNE. THE CHOICE IS YOURS.

IF YOU SHOOT HIM, I'LL SHOOT YOU. IF YOU TRY TO AIM THE GUN AT ME, I'LL SHOOT YOU.
BUDDA BUDDA
SO YOU EITHER GIVE UP OR PRAY THAT I MISS.
AND I *WON'T* MISS.
21

I thank him for saving my life. Again.

FORGET IT. SEE YOU TOMORROW NIGHT.

POLICE

WIN ORIGINAL BATMAN ADVENTURES ART!
DETAILS INSIDE!
APPROVED BY THE COMICS CODE AUTHORITY
DC
6
US $1.25
CAN $1.60
UK 70p
THE BATMAN ADVENTURES
fox kids network
TM
PUCKETT,
OBECK
RCHETT
S.S.
BOOM! YOU'RE DEAD!

THE KILLING BOOK
ACT ONE:
SEDUCTION OF THE INNOCENT!
BOHA-WHADOOOM
KELLEY PUCKETT WRITER
MIKE PAROBECK PENCILLER
RICK BURCHETT INKER
RICK TAYLOR COLORIST
TIM HARKINS LETTERER
DARREN VINCENZO ASS'T ED.
SCOTT PETERSON EDITOR
BATMAN CREATED BY BOB KANE

JOKER.

WELL, THAT WAS FUN!
TH-THESE IS ALL OF BATMAN'S C-COSTUME PIECES WE COULD F-FIND, B-BOSS.

WHAT? THIS WON'T FILL UP TWO PAGES OF MY SCRAPBOOK!
KEEP LOOKING!
TOLD YA IT WAS HIM.

OH, LOOK! CHILDREN! TWO LOVELY, YOUNG DEFENSELESS CHILDREN!
HE'S THE JOKER. THE GUY BATMAN ALWAYS BEATS.

"THE GUY BATMAN ALWAYS..."
WHY, YOU POOR, DELUDED CHILD. WHEREVER DID YOU GET THAT IDEA?
GOTHAM ADVENTURES
I READ IT HERE.
3

WHAT?!
GOTHAM ADVENTURES
SPECIAL GUEST ARTIST ANTHONY BALDWIN!

COME ON! WE'RE LEAVING!
THE NERVE! FILLING YOUNGSTERS' HEADS WITH VICIOUS LIES...IMPUGNING MY GOOD NAME... MISREPRESENTING ME TO AMERICA'S YOUTH!

WELL, WE'LL JUST SEE ABOUT THIS! I'M GOING TO SET THE RECORD STRAIGHT AND I WON'T REST UNTIL THE JOB IS DONE! BECAUSE THIS TIME...

...I'M DOING IT FOR THE CHILDREN!
LOLLIPOP, ANYONE?

YER FIRED!
MR. PATTERSON WOULD LIKE TO THANK YOU FOR YOUR EFFORTS AND WISH YOU THE BEST OF LUCK IN YOUR FUTURE ASSIGNMENTS.

UH... MR. PATTERSON? WHY'D YOU JUST FIRE THE REGULAR GOTHAM ADVENTURES TEAM?
WHY?! HAVE YOU SEEN THE NUMBERS ON YOUR FILL-IN ISSUE?!
BOSS!
CREATIVE DIFFERENCES, ANTHONY. YOU'LL BE DOING GOTHAM ADVENTURES FROM NOW ON.

BUT I JUST DRAW! I CAN'T WRITE.
"WRITE"?! IT'S A COMIC BOOK! CRAZY KIDS...
MR. PATTERSON'S SURE YOUR TALENT WILL CARRY YOU THROUGH, ANTHONY.

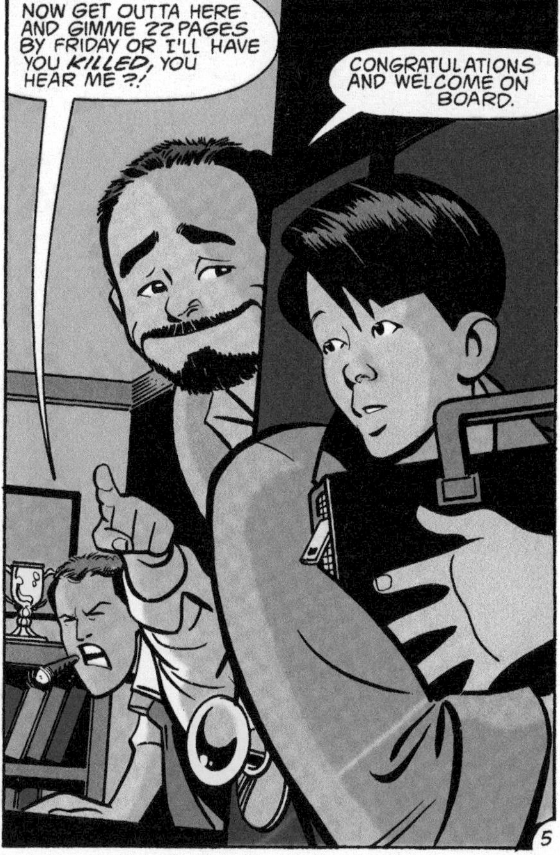
NOW GET OUTTA HERE AND GIMME 22 PAGES BY FRIDAY OR I'LL HAVE YOU KILLED, YOU HEAR ME?!
CONGRATULATIONS AND WELCOME ON BOARD.
5

ICE CREAM! BOMB POPS!
HEY, KID! HOW ABOUT SOME ICE CREAM?
ICE CREAM? BUT IT'S FREEZING OUT HERE.
WELL, THEN--HOW ABOUT A VIOLENT ABDUCTION INSTEAD?
HEY!
OH, WHAT THE HECK. TAKE BOTH. MY TREAT.
IT IS THE SEASON OF GIVING, AFTER ALL.
BOY, I JUST CAN'T SAY NO TO KIDS.
ICE CREAM! BOMB POPS! PENCILLERS!

...BEEN MISSING FOR OVER A WEEK. YOU SAY YOU HAVEN'T SEEN HIM SINCE HE LEFT YOUR OFFICE?
YOU CALLING ME A LIAR?!
REGRETFULLY, NO, OFFICER MONTOYA. WE'VE NEITHER SEEN NOR HEARD FROM HIM.
THE KING

THE LAST OF THOSE ANTHONY BALDWIN PAGES JUST ARRIVED, MISTER PATTERSON.
WHAT? I THOUGHT YOU SAID YOU HAVEN'T HEARD FROM HIM!

YOU CAN'T PIN NOTHING ON ME, COPPER!
YOU SEE, ANTHONY'S BEEN SENDING ARTWORK IN FOR THE PAST TWO DAYS, BUT HE HASN'T CONTACTED US OTHERWISE.
MONTOYA. YOU BETTER TAKE A LOOK AT THIS.

BUT THIS... SATURDAY NIGHT'S... HOW...?
7

# ACT 2: HOW TO DRAW COMICS · · THE JOKER WAY

INTERNATIONAL CRYPTOGRAPHERS CONVENTION
...SEEM UNGRATEFUL, BUT THIS SOUP TASTES A LITTLE... OFF.
MON DIEU! SOMEONE HAS TAMPERED WITH MY SOUP!
YOU! WHAT HAVE YOU DONE TO MY SOUP?! IT TASTES...HOW YOU SAY...
...POISONOUS? THAT WOULD BE THE POISON. IT COMPLEMENTS THE CILANTRO NICELY, DON'T YOU THINK?
POISON?! WHA--
SACRE BLEU! LE JOKER!
YES, IT'S A SAVORY LITTLE PARALYTIC MIXTURE WHICH SHOULD HIT YOU RIGHT ABOUT...
...NOW.
MUCH BETTER.
THUD
9

GOSH! MY ARRIVAL'S SO UNEXPECTED... I HOPE THEY'RE HAPPY TO SEE ME!
AH! THEY LIKE ME! THEY REALLY LIKE ME!
DON'T WORRY, FELLAS. I DIDN'T COME EMPTY-HANDED!
10

PLEASE. DON'T GET UP. IT'S THE LEAST I COULD DO.
BONK
HEY!
SSHHH! YOU WANNA BREAK HIS CONCENTRATION?
THIS MAN IS AN ARTIST!
11

FORE!
BONK

YOU'LL NEVER GROW UP TO BE A BIG STRONG CRYPTOGRAPHER IF YOU DON'T FINISH YOUR VEGGIES!
BONK

Hmmm.

WHOOSH
12

INTERNATIONAL CRYPTOGRAPHERS CONVENTION
I HOPE YOU APPRECIATE THE MESSAGE, BATSY! IT TOOK THE GREATEST HEADS IN CRYPTOGRAPHY TO BRING IT TO YOU.
BE THERE...
...OR ELSE.
THE END???
13
THE CRYPTOGRAPHERS' INJURIES RANGED FROM BROKEN NOSES TO HEAVY CONCUSSIONS, BUT THEY'LL ALL RECOVER.

AND THIS "MESSAGE" HE REFERS TO?
MORSE CODE. THE CRYPTOGRAPHERS' HEADS REPRESENT DOTS-- THE FEET REPRESENT DASHES. IT GIVES AN ADDRESS AND A TIME. IT HAPPENS TONIGHT.

NEED I EVEN ASK IF YOU'VE INFORMED THE POLICE?
NO. HOSTAGE... SITUATION...
...TOO... UNPREDICTABLE... DANGEROUS...

THEN IT'S CERTAINLY TOO DANGEROUS FOR YOU. YOU'RE WEAK, YOUR REACTIONS ARE SLUGGISH, YOUR TIMING IS OFF.
I MANAGED TO DEFLECT THE KNIVES, DIDN'T I?

YOU WERE TRYING TO CATCH THEM, SIR.
READY THE CAR, ALFRED. I'M GOING.
14

# ACT 3: COMICS AND SEQUENTIAL

POOM
COMFORTABLE, BATMAN?
I REALIZE THAT BEING CHAINED TO AN EXPLODING ROCKET TRIGGERED BY A GOLF BALL IS A SILLY WAY TO DIE, BUT HEY--THAT'S COMICS!
16

AND A HUSH FALLS OVER THE CROWD AS HE STARTS HIS SWING...

P-TANG

YOU BOYS DON'T MIND IF I TAKE A "MULLIGAN" ON THAT ONE, DO YOU?

DOINK

TOUGHER THAN IT LOOKS.

PTOW

GRRRR

THUD

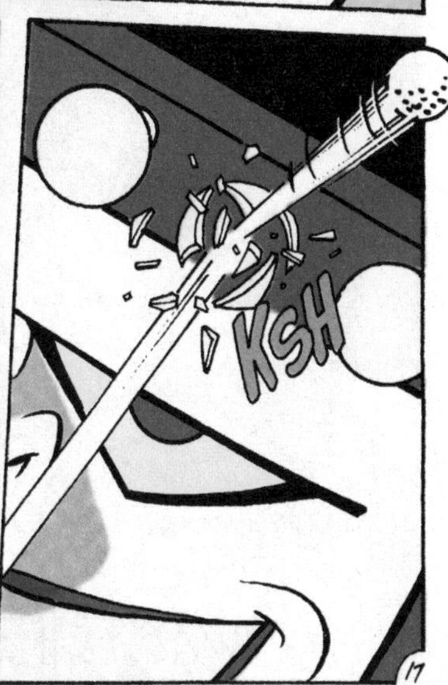
KSH
17

ENOUGH! I'M ENDING THIS NOW, BEFORE I RUN OUT OF...
... ER... SUPPLIES.

BON VOYAGE, BAT--
--MAN.?

BONK
BUDDA BUDDA

BUDDA BUDDA BUDDA
I CAN'T SEE HIM! IT'S TOO DARK!
BONK
18

BONK
BUDDA

ENOUGH FOOLING AROUND, BATMAN. COME OUT OR THE BRAT GETS IT.
LET THE BOY GO, JOKER. I'LL COME OUT AS SOON AS YOU LET THE BOY GO.

YOU'LL COME OUT ANYWAY. NOW STOP WASTING TIME--

ANTHONY! GET OUT OF HERE AND CALL THE POLICE!
--GGK!
19

THOK

KRAK

WHAM

THAT EXPLOSION TOOK A LOT OUT OF YOU, DIDN'T IT, BATSY?
THIS ISN'T THE WAY I WANTED TO END IT, BUT ANY PORT IN A STORM...!
20

BATMAN!

WHUMP

AAAAAAHH!
WHOOSH

OWOWOWOWOW
21

HOW MANY OF THESE THINGS ARE THERE?
ONE FOR EVERY INMATE. SOME RICH GUY DONATED 'EM ALL -- SOME KIND OF LITERACY CAMPAIGN.
HA HA
HA HA
LITERACY? IT'S JUST A COMIC BOOK, RIGHT?
YEAH, BUT IT MADE 'EM ALL LAUGH.
WELL, *ALMOST* ALL OF 'EM.
HA HA HA HA HA
THAT IS *NOT FUNNY* !!!
HA HA HA
HA HA
THE END

WIN ORIGINAL BATMAN ADVENTURES ART!
DETAILS INSIDE!
APPROVED BY THE COMICS CODE AUTHORITY
$1.50 US
$1.95 CAN
70p UK
94
fox kids network
THE
BY PUCKETT
PAROBECK
& BURCHETT

THE TANGLED WEB
EDWARD CORDERO!
ACT I:
KELLEY PUCKETT WRITER
MIKE PAROBECK PENCILLER
RICK BURCHETT INKER
RICK TAYLOR COLORIST
DARREN VINCENZO ASSISTANT BEDOUIN
STARKINGS/ COMICRAFT LETTERING
SCOTT PETERSON GRAND POOBAH
BATMAN CREATED BY BOB KANE
INTO THE SHADOWS

KRAK

WELCOME BACK TO GOTHAM, FAST EDDIE.

EXIT
I'VE BEEN WAITING A LONG TIME TO GET MY HANDS ON YOU.
GOTHAM INTER
2

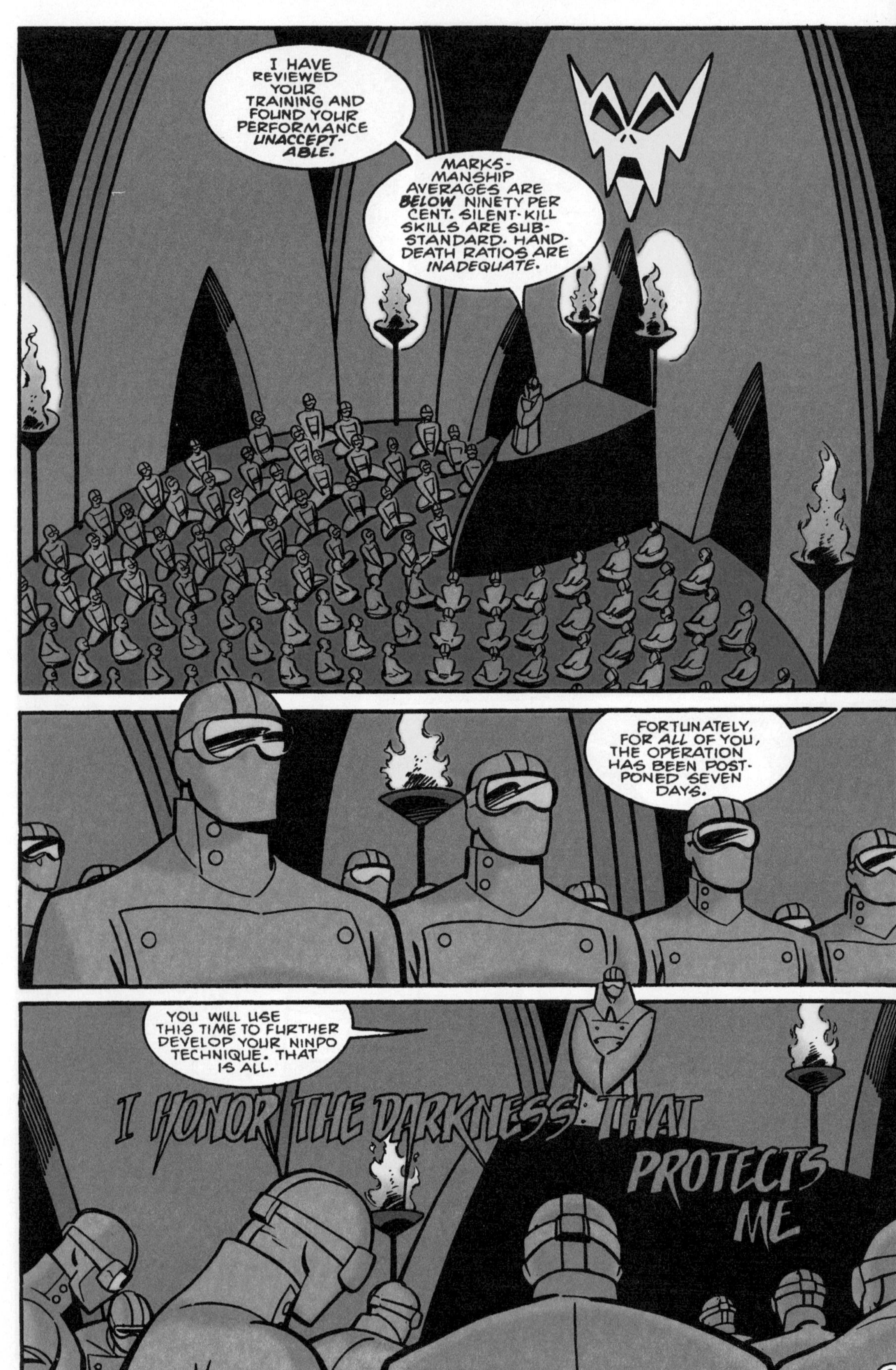
I HAVE REVIEWED YOUR TRAINING AND FOUND YOUR PERFORMANCE UNACCEPT-ABLE.
MARKS-MANSHIP AVERAGES ARE BELOW NINETY PER CENT. SILENT-KILL SKILLS ARE SUB-STANDARD. HAND-DEATH RATIOS ARE INADEQUATE.
FORTUNATELY, FOR ALL OF YOU, THE OPERATION HAS BEEN POST-PONED SEVEN DAYS.
YOU WILL USE THIS TIME TO FURTHER DEVELOP YOUR NINPO TECHNIQUE. THAT IS ALL.
I HONOR THE DARKNESS THAT PROTECTS ME
3

ALFRED.

ALFRED. COME IN.

-:- Ahem -:- THE BLACKBIRD CROWS AT MIDNIGHT.
VERY FUNNY. NOW LISTEN CAREFULLY -- THIS TRANSMISSION WILL BE PICKED UP IF IT LASTS MUCH LONGER THAN SIXTY SECONDS.

OUR EXHAUSTIVE ANALYSIS OF THAT MICROFILM INFORMATION PAID OFF. RA'S AL GHUL HAS ESTABLISHED A MAJOR OPERATION HERE.
AND THE GOAL OF THIS "OPERATION..?"
4

RA'S HAS ONLY ONE GOAL -- TO FORCIBLY RESTORE THE ECOLOGICAL BALANCE OF THE PLANET BY WIPING OUT MOST OF CIVILIZATION.
BUT I DON'T KNOW HOW HE PLANS TO DO IT.

HAVE THE COMPUTER SCAN FOR NUCLEAR REACTORS, BIOLOGICAL WEAPON LABORATORIES, SENSITIVE PLATE TECTONICS -- ANYTHING WITHIN A HUNDRED-MILE RADIUS CAPABLE OF BEING USED FOR DESTRUCTION ON A GLOBAL SCALE.

"SCANNING"
I DON'T SUPPOSE YOU'LL BE WITHDRAWING TO A SAFE LOCATION WHILE AWAITING THE RESULTS?
NO. THERE'S SOMETHING ABOUT THIS WHOLE SETUP THAT DOESN'T SEEM QUITE RIGHT.

IN ALL MY YEARS OF BATTLING RA'S AL GHUL, I'VE NEVER HEARD OF ONE OF HIS OPERATIONS BEING DELAYED...
AND THAT IS?

I CANNOT IMPRESS UPON YOU ENOUGH THE IMPORTANCE OF INFORMING EVERY-ONE OF THE DELAY.
I INFORMED THEM MYSELF NOT THREE HOURS AGO, AL GHUL. NOW, WON'T YOU PLEASE RECONSIDER?

I COULD ENSURE THE SUCCESS OF OUR MISSION IF ONLY I KNEW WHAT THE TARGET WAS. AS IT IS NOW--
DO NOT BE CONCERNED. I HAVE FAITH THAT YOU WILL AC-QUIT YOURSELF WELL WHEN THE TIME COMES.

AS TO THE OTHER MATTER...?
WE CON-TINUE TO SEARCH FOR EVIDENCE OF THE BATMAN'S INVOLVE-MENT, BUT HAVE FOUND NOTHING. MAY I ASK WHY YOU ARE SO CER-TAIN HE WILL APPEAR?

BECAUSE I HAVE MADE CERTAIN.
6

ACT II: NEW WORLD ORDER
EXPLAIN YOURSELF, MISTER ASQUITH.
THE DELAY WAS UNFORESEEABLE, MY LORD. I'D CONTRACTED A FORCE OF DEEP-DESERT BEDOUINS TO SECURE THE AREA ON SCHEDULE, BUT NOW THEY CLAIM THEY HAVE TO WAIT --
ONE WEEK TO CELEBRATE THE FEAST OF UZAIR. THE HOLIDAY IS WELL-KNOWN IN THAT REGION -- A CHILD ON THE STREET COULD HAVE TOLD YOU OF IT.
SURELY I CAN'T BE EXPECTED TO KNOW EVERY-THING...
AT LEAST HAVE THE DECENCY TO BE ASHAMED OF YOUR IGNORANCE!
MERCY, MY LORD-- HAVE MERCY!
GO. RETURN TO AFRICA AND PRAY THAT YOUR INCOMPETENCE HAS NOT COST YOU YOUR LIFE.
7

...BEEN ALL THROUGH THE COMPLEX AND THE SURROUNDING AREA. THE MISSION IS TOMORROW NIGHT AND I STILL DON'T KNOW WHAT THEIR TARGET IS.
PERHAPS THEY'VE REGAINED THEIR SANITY AND CALLED IT OFF.
NOT LIKELY.
WE'VE BEEN TALKING LONG ENOUGH, ALFRED. I'M SIGNING OFF NOW. WISH ME LUCK.
SIR! WE'VE PICKED UP A TRANSMISSION FROM INSIDE THE PERIMETER. THEY STOPPED SENDING ALMOST IMMEDIATELY...
...BUT WE WERE ABLE TO TRACK THE TARGET DESTINATION. IT WAS SENT TO GOTHAM CITY. THE BATMAN IS HERE.
EXCELLENT. THE TIME HAS COME TO FULLY INFORM YOU OF YOUR MISSION. LISTEN CLOSELY...
8

GREETINGS, MY LORD. HOW WAS YOUR FLIGHT?
SHOW ME THE EQUIPMENT.
AS YOU CAN SEE, IT'S FULLY ASSEMBLED. FINAL TESTING WILL BE COMPLETED VERY SOON. COMM LINKS ARE ALREADY ON-LINE.
GOOD. SECURITY?
WELL, THE BEDOUINS HAVE STATIONED THEMSELVES AROUND THE PERIMETER, BUT WE'RE AT LEAST A HUNDRED MILES FROM CIVILIZATION, SO I'M NOT SURE HOW NECESSARY...
9

AND WHO IS THIS?
Eh--? HE'S JUST ONE OF THE BED --

I SEE BY YOUR SWORD THAT YOU HAVE STUDIED WITH ZABUR EL-SHAITAN. YOUR SKILLS WILL BE WASTED HERE, I THINK. I DO NOT ANTICIPATE COMBAT.
ONE SHOULD ALWAYS ANTICIPATE COMBAT, DREAD ONE.
QUITE SO. DO NOT LET ME DISTURB YOU FURTHER.
YOU HONOR ME WITH YOUR ATTENTION.

EVERYTHING SEEMS TO BE IN ORDER.
CONGRATULATIONS, ASQUITH. YOU WILL LIVE TO SEE THE DAWN.
10

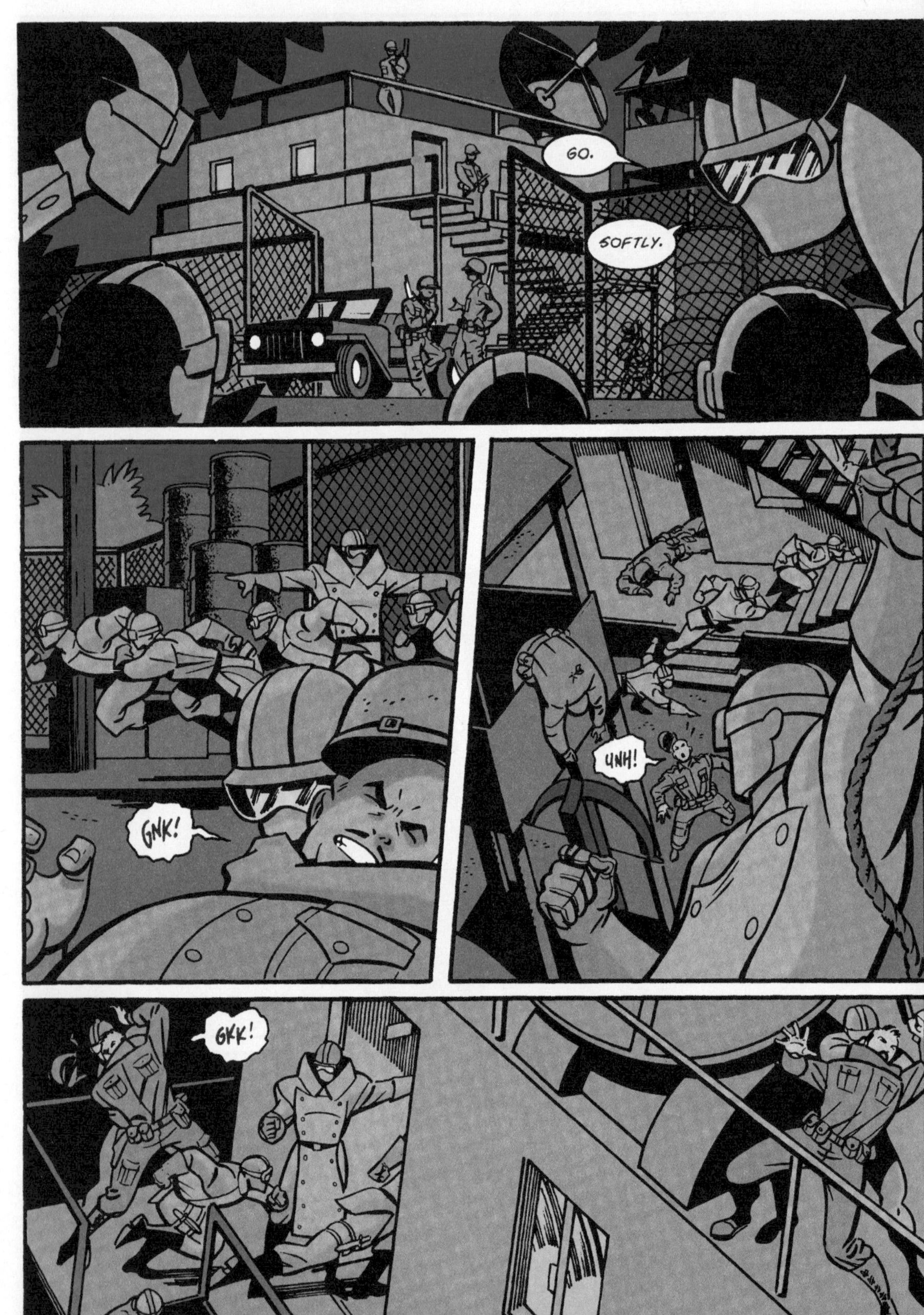
GO.
SOFTLY.
GNK!
UNH!
GKK!
11

THE ROOM IS SECURED, LEADER.
GOOD. AND NOW...

BEEP
BEEP
BEEP
...IT'S AN HONOR TO FINALLY MEET YOU...

...BATMAN!
COME. OUR LORD WISHES TO SPEAK WITH YOU.
12

GREETINGS, DETECTIVE. YOU MUST PARDON MY "DECOY" OPERATION -- I COULD NOT RUN THE RISK OF YOUR INTERFERING WITH MY PLANS YET AGAIN.
I WANT YOU TO UNDERSTAND WHAT I AM ABOUT TO DO.

OVER THE PAST SEVERAL MONTHS, I HAVE INSTALLED A LARGE CHAIN OF EXPLOSIVES IN THE VERY HEART OF THE ANTARCTIC POLAR REGION.
I SHALL SEND THE DESTRUCT SIGNAL THROUGH THIS CONSOLE VIA SATELLITE.

ONCE DETONATED, THESE BOMBS WILL SET A SIGNIFICANT PORTION OF THE GLACIERS ADRIFT. THEY WILL BE INEXORABLY DRAWN INTO THE WARMER WATERS OF THE OCEAN WHERE THEY WILL MELT.

WATER LEVELS WILL RISE ACROSS THE GLOBE. THE COASTAL AREAS OF EVERY CONTINENT WILL BE COMPLETELY SUBMERGED. THE MAJOR INDUSTRIAL CENTERS OF THE WORLD WILL BE DESTROYED.
13

MILLIONS... BILLIONS WILL LOSE THEIR LIVES.
BUT THOSE WHO REMAIN WILL WATCH AS THE EARTH CLEANSES HERSELF OF MANKIND'S TOXINS. HER FRAGILE ECOSYSTEMS WILL REGAIN THEIR BALANCE. THE WORLD SHALL BE RENEWED.

THIS PLACE WHERE I STAND NOW --
-- THE MOST BARREN, LIFE-LESS AREA OF THE GLOBE -- WILL, WITHIN ONE GENER-ATION BECOME A GARDEN PARADISE BECAUSE OF WHAT I DO THIS DAY.

I WILL NOT ASK YOU AGAIN TO JOIN ME -- I WELL KNOW YOUR OB-JECTIONS TO MY METHODS.
BUT I WILL KEEP YOU ALIVE, DETECTIVE.
THE NEW WORLD WILL NEED MEN LIKE YOU.
14

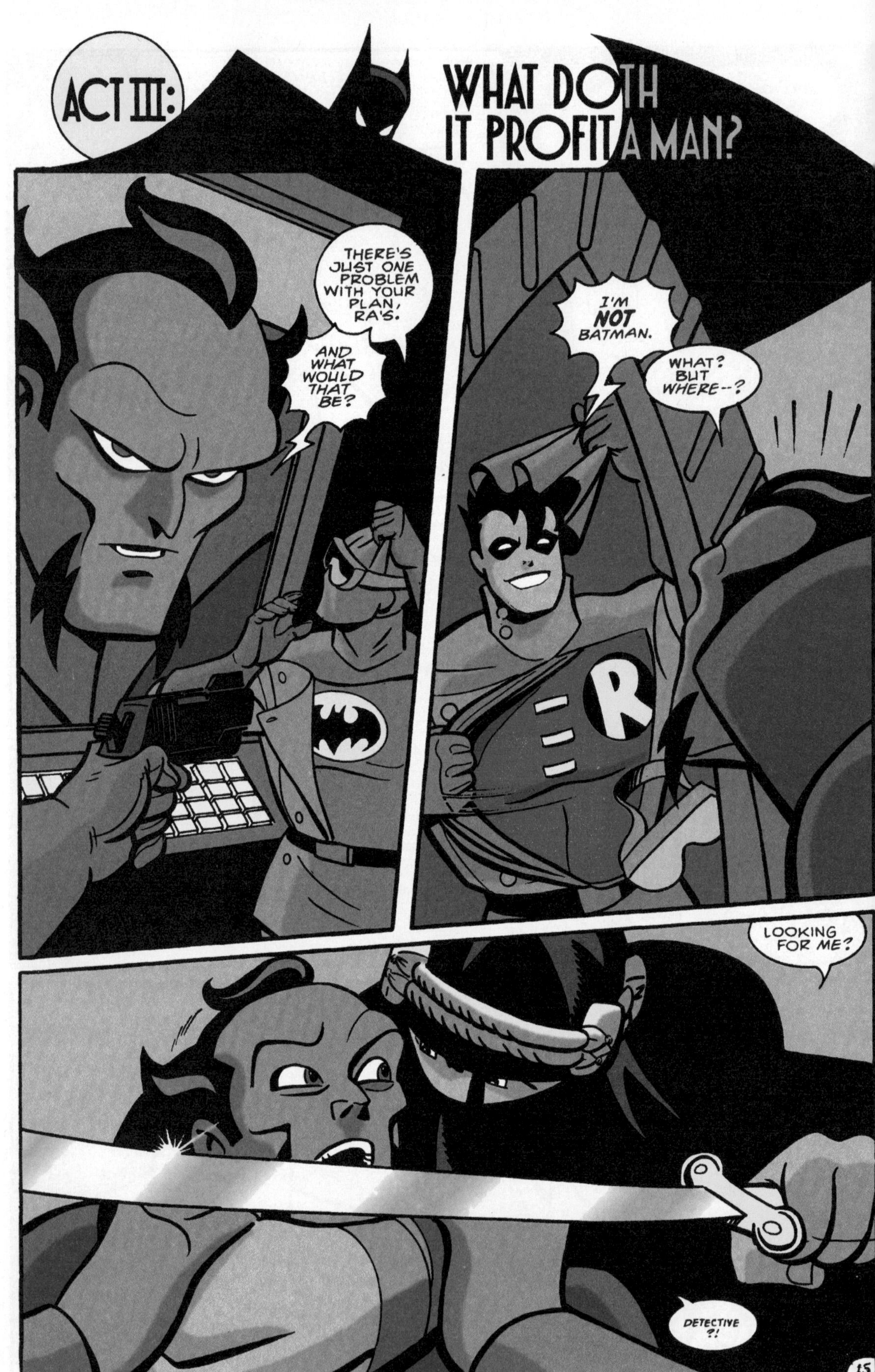
ACT III:
WHAT DOTH IT PROFIT A MAN?
THERE'S JUST ONE PROBLEM WITH YOUR PLAN, RA'S.
AND WHAT WOULD THAT BE?
I'M NOT BATMAN.
WHAT? BUT WHERE--?
LOOKING FOR ME?
DETECTIVE ?!
15

ALL OF YOU -- THROW DOWN YOUR GUNS.

THE ROBES? THE SWORD?
ALI-YASA WASN'T EL-SHAITAN'S ONLY STUDENT.
HE WASN'T THE BEST EITHER.

NOBODY MOVE OR AL GHUL DIES.
HE'S BLUF-NNNGK!
16

AL GHUL WILL REWARD ME GREATLY FOR THIS...
SKRAKK
...THEN AGAIN, MAYBE NOT.
17

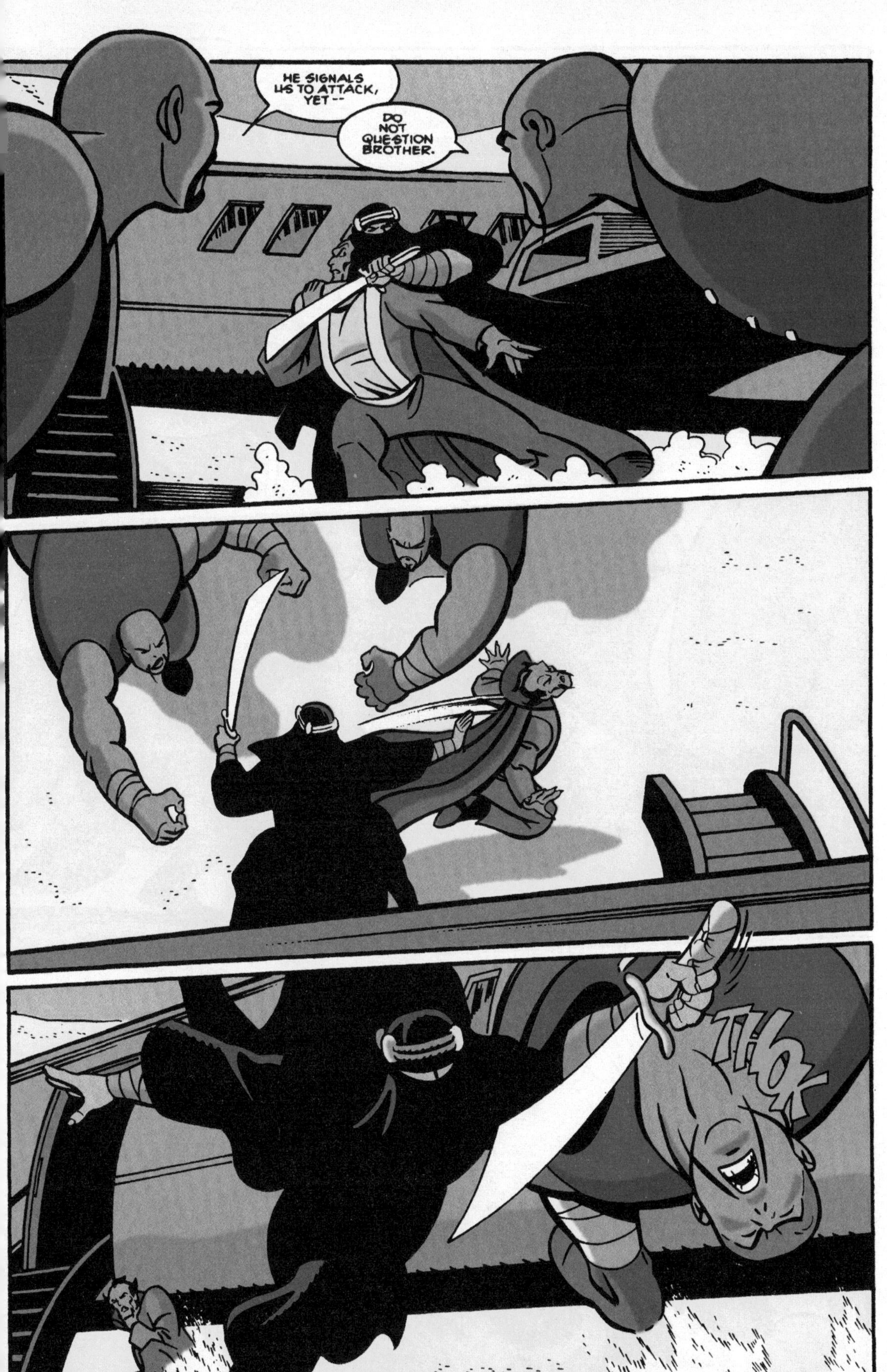
HE SIGNALS US TO ATTACK, YET --
DO NOT QUESTION BROTHER.
THOK
18

WHAT ARE YOU DOING?! WHY AREN'T YOU ATTACKING HIM?!
EITHER HE IS THE GREAT ALI-YASA, OR HE HAS DEFEATED THE GREAT ALI-YASA.
ANY MAN WHO ATTACKS HIM IS A FOOL.
BLAM! BLAM!
COWARDS. I --
THAK
BLAM
19

WHOOSH
20

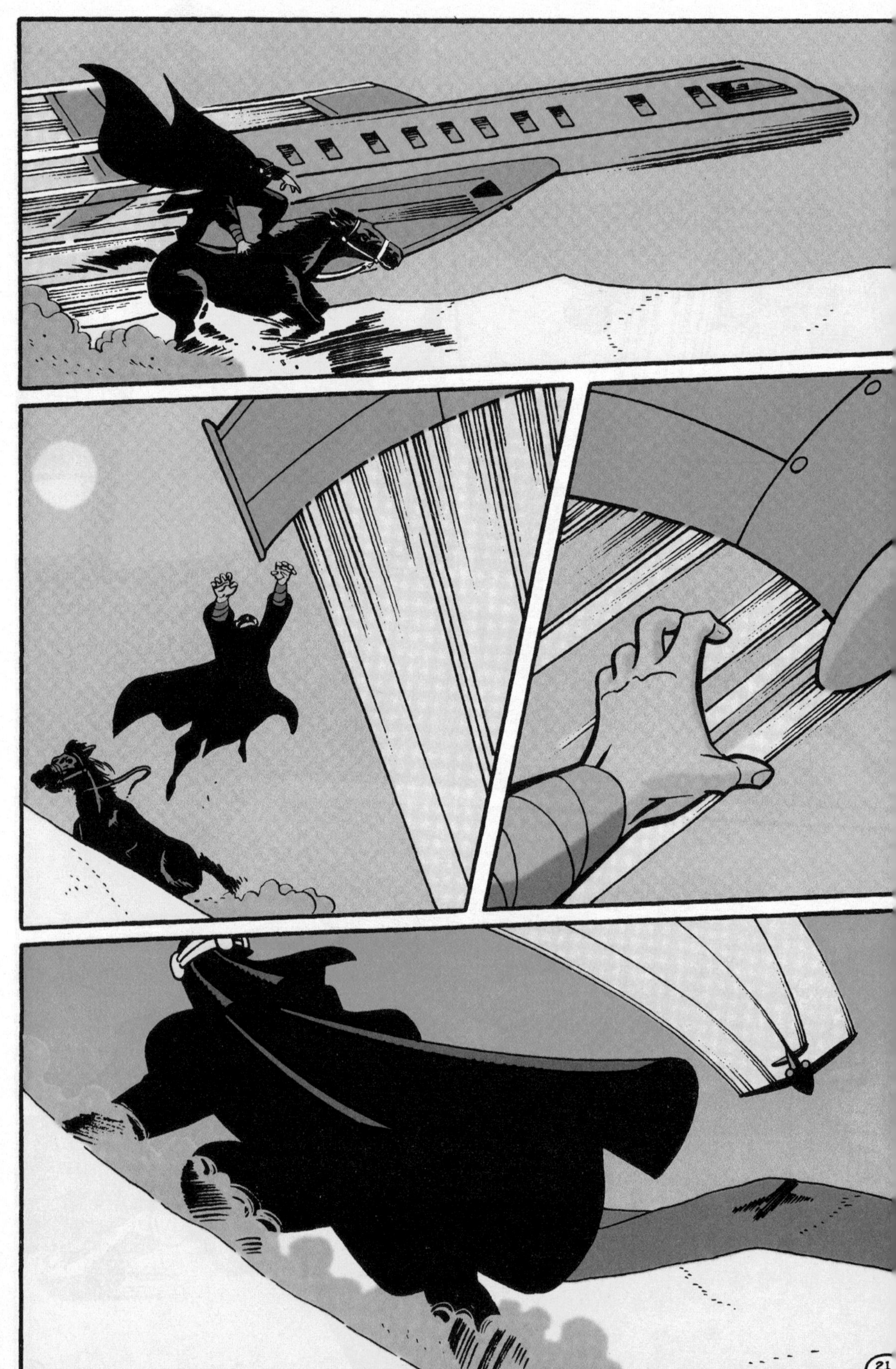
21

THE BOY DEFEATED US AND ESCAPED, AL GHUL. I OFFER MY LIFE IN PAYMENT FOR MY FAILURE.
THE FAILURE WAS MINE. I SHOULD HAVE RECOGNIZED THE INFLUENCE OF EL-SHAITAN ON THE DETECTIVE'S SWORDPLAY.

HAD I DONE SO, I COULD HAVE ANTICIPATED HIS FAMILIARITY WITH THE FEAST OF UZAIR.
YOU HAVE DONE WELL. RETURN TO TIBET AND AWAIT MY INSTRUCTIONS.
MY LORD.

I WONDER, DETECTIVE -- WHAT ARE YOU THINKING NOW, AT YOUR HOUSE ON THE HILL?
ARE YOU THINKING ABOUT THE LIVES YOU HAVE SAVED ..?

"...OR ARE YOU CONSIDERING THE WORLD THAT MIGHT HAVE BEEN?"
THE END

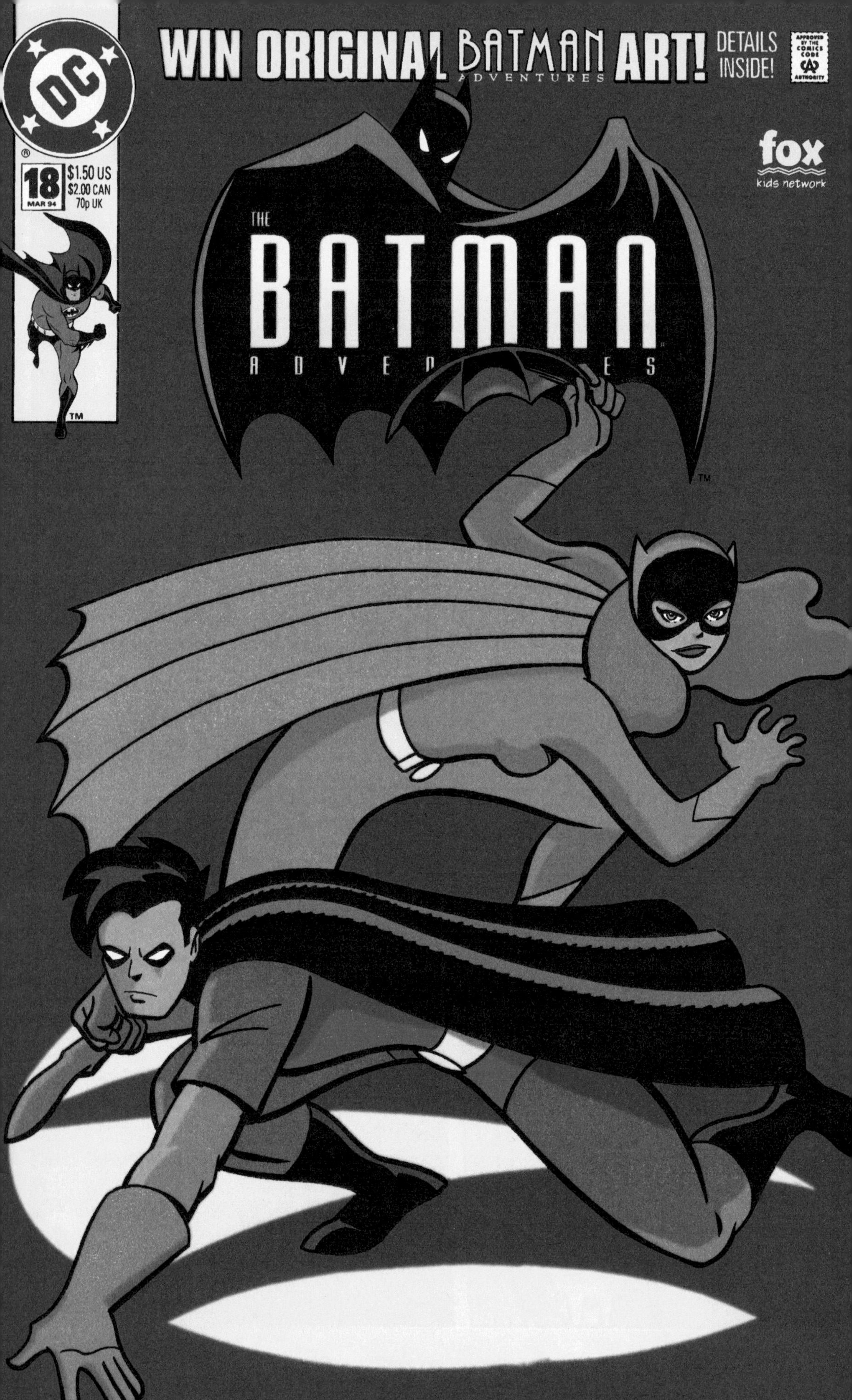
WIN ORIGINAL BATMAN ADVENTURES ART! DETAILS INSIDE!
DC
18
MAR 94
$1.50 US
$2.00 CAN
70p UK
THE BATMAN ADVENTURES
fox kids network

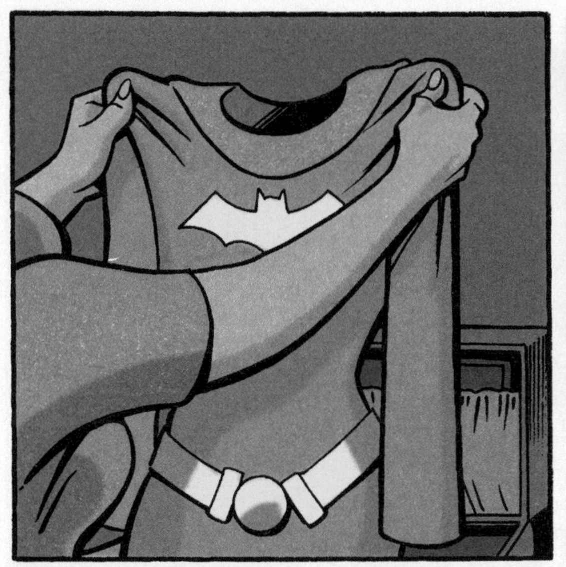

TIK
TIK

CLASS SCHEDULE
GOTHAM UNIVERSITY

TIK
TIK

GOTHA
CLIK
CLIK

CLIK
CLIK
1

DECISION DAY
ACT I: EYEWITNESS!
I'M SORRY, HONEY. I'LL JUST BE ANOTHER FIFTEEN MINUTES.
S'OKAY, DAD. I CAN WAIT.
KELLEY PUCKETT WRITER
MIKE PAROBECK PENCILLER
RICK BURCHETT INKER
RICK TAYLOR COLORIST
DARREN VINCENZO ASSISTANT EDITOR
STARKINGS/ COMICRAFT LETTERING
SCOTT PETERSON EDITOR
BATMAN CREATED BY BOB KANE

I'LL SAY IT ONE MORE TIME: FIRST YOU TURN ON YOUR SIRENS...
WANTED BABYFACE BILL O'NER
WANTED NITRATE NINA POWELL

... THEN YOU TRY TO PULL 'EM OVER. GOT IT?
WANTED STARSHINE ROWELL
WANTED YOUSHKA DAJANI

GOOD LUCK WITH THE NOSE, CHET.
DANKS.
THAT BRIEF-CASE...

HEY, WAIT!
3

HEY, MISTER! YOU DROPPED YOUR...
...BRIEF-CASE.
GET IN HERE, YOU IDIOT! IT'S GOING TO BLOW!
"BLOW"?!
4

WHAT'S SHE DOING?
DOESN'T MATTER.
BOOM
SHE WON'T BE IDENTIFYING ANYONE SOON.
5

NO! THE MOMENT YOUR DAUGHTER IDENTIFIES OUR BOMBER FROM THE MUG SHOTS, I WANT HIM ARRESTED, CHARGED AND INCARCERATED!
BUT HE WASN'T ACTING ALONE! OUR PRIORITY IS TO CONVICT WHO-EVER PLANNED THE BOMBING--
OUR PRIORITY, MS. ASSISTANT DISTRICT ATTORNEY, IS TO SHOW SOMEONE BEING PUNISHED FOR THIS CRIME BEFORE WE'RE ALL VOTED OUT OF OFFICE NEXT WEEK!
IF BOB HEWLETT WINS THE ELECTION, WE ALL GO. HE'S ALREADY GROOMING GRIFFIN FOR GORDON'S JOB.
DON'T YOU GET IT? BARBARA'S TESTIMONY IS THE ONLY EVIDENCE AGAINST THIS GUY. LET ME GET SOMETHING ELSE ON HIM. ANYTHING.
IF I DON'T... I CAN'T GUARANTEE MY DAUGHTER'S SAFETY.
SORRY, GORDON. THAT WOULD TAKE TIME-- TIME WE DON'T HAVE.
BRING HIM IN IMMEDIATELY. IF YOU DON'T, I'LL FIND SOMEONE WHO WILL.
COMMISSIONER... YOU'RE NOT GOING TO DO IT, ARE YOU?
PUT A DEATH WARRANT ON MY DAUGHTER'S HEAD IN ORDER TO KEEP MY JOB? WHAT DO YOU THINK?
6

HOW ABOUT THESE? RECOGNIZE ANY OF THEM?

NO.
9-2122
P^F #4909-2123

YOU CAN SLEEP HERE, SWEETIE. I'LL MAKE SURE NOBODY DISTURBS YOU.
TRY TO GET SOME REST, OKAY?
I WILL, DADDY.

*TOMORROW* NIGHT.
7

# ACT II: SMOKING GUN

WELL, I KNOW HE'S THE ONE, SO HE MUST HAVE BUILT THE BOMB SOME-PLACE ELSE.
LET'S SHADOW HIM, THEN.
Er, THAT IS, IF YOU'D LIKE TO WORK TOGETHER ...

THAT WOULD BE GREAT, ROBIN. I COULD USE THE HELP.
COOL. SO WHAT'S OUR NEXT--

WAITA-SECOND

HEY, THERE HE IS! HE JUST CAME OUT.
WE CAN'T LEAVE JUST YET, BATGIRL...

...WE'VE GOT TROUBLE.
9

I'LL TAKE CARE OF THIS.
YOU BUG TELLER'S CAR BEFORE HE GETS AWAY. *DEAL?*
Uhh, *SURE,* BUT...

...HOW?

NOT GOING TO MAKE IT -- HE'S GETTING AWAY...

10

OOOF
COME ON, COME ON...
UNH!
HEY! YOU ALL RIGHT?
11

HE'S GOT THE WINDOW COVERED ...

...BUT IT LOOKS LIKE HE'S DOWN IN THE BASE-MENT.
-TSK- THIS WINDOW'S LOCKED.

SEE, I DIDN'T THINK THERE WAS ROOM IN THAT BELT TO HOLD LOCKPICKS. WHAT DO YOU NORMALLY DO, JUST FORCE IT?
Umm... YEAH. I JUST FORCE IT.

THAT'S COOL.
LOOK, I DIDN'T MEAN ANYTHING BY THAT LOCKPICK COMMENT...
ROBIN, HOW LONG DID YOU HAVE TO TRAIN BEFORE YOU STARTED BEING ROBIN?

ABOUT SIX, SEVEN YEARS. WHY?
JUST WONDERING.
12

WHA--?

THIS IS *EXACTLY* WHAT I NEEDED!
CLIK
WHAT ARE YOU--? *LEMME GO!*

THE *POLICE?*
LET ME *GO!*
EEOOOEEEOOOEEEOOOEE

I CONFESS! I DID THE WHOLE THING! YOU'VE GOT ME *DEAD TO RIGHTS!*

HE SEEMED A LITTLE *EAGER* TO GIVE HIM-SELF UP, DIDN'T HE?
WHO'S THAT OVER *THERE?*
13

...COMING TO YOU LIVE WITH THE MAN RESPONSIBLE FOR THE "COP BOMBER" ARREST, JEFF GRIFFIN.
THANK YOU, SUMMER. I WAS OUTRAGED BY THE ATTEMPTED BOMBING, SO I LOOKED INTO THE CASE AND WAS ABLE TO HELP THE POLICE FIND THEIR MAN.
G

ISN'T THAT A LITTLE CONVENIENT? THE MAN AFTER DA-- COMMISSIONER GORDON'S JOB JUST HAPPENING TO CATCH THE BOMBER?
AND WHAT ABOUT TELLER? I'VE NEVER SEEN ANY-ONE THAT EAGER FOR JAIL TIME.

--SOME-THING OF A COINCIDENCE?
I'D BE HAPPY TO ANSWER THAT QUESTION LATER, MS. GLEASON, BUT I SEE THAT A GOOD FRIEND OF MINE HAS JUST ARRIVED.
LADIES AND GENTLE-MEN, THE NEXT MAJOR OF GOTHAM CITY...

...BOB HEWLETT!
CLIK
CLIK
Oh, BOY.
14

ACT III:
NO JUSTICE, NO PEACE!
HAVE A GOOD SHIFT, BUDDY! DON'T LET ANYBODY ESCAPE!
WHAT?!
Oh. HA HA. THAT'S A GOOD ONE.

I... I'M ONLY DOING THIS BECAUSE I NEED THE MONEY FOR--
WHATEVER.

TELLER! LET'S GO!

A MILLION BUCKS AND A TICKET TO ASIA. YOU'RE SITTIN' PRETTY, TELLER.
ASIA
15

JUST STASH THAT CASH AND DROP OUTTA--
YIKES!
THUMP
KKRSSH
16

BLAM
BLAM
BLAM
BLAM
THOK
THOK
BLAM
WHAK
17

IT'S OVER! IT'S ALL OVER!

VOTE
GET HOLD OF YOURSELF. TELL ME WHAT HAPPENED.
IT WAS ROBIN! HE ATTACKED US JUST OUTSIDE THE STATION! I GOT AWAY, BUT HE GOT THE OTHERS AND THE MONEY!

LISTEN TO ME -- THE OTHERS HAVE A COVER STORY, BUT YOU'VE GOT TO DISAPPEAR. I'M GOING TO GIVE YOU SOME MONEY AND YOU'RE GOING TO GET ON THAT FLIGHT TO ASIA, GOT IT?

GET THE PETTY CASH, GRIFFIN.

WHAT'S IMPORTANT IS THAT YOU REMAIN CALM. ONCE YOU'RE ON THAT PLANE YOU'LL BE SAFE, ALL RIGHT? OKAY?
YES, SIR. THANK YOU.
18

GOTCHA.

HEY, YOU!
STAGE DOOR

GET HER!

19

NOW, WAIT ONE MINUTE, YOUNG LADY--
20

... BUT, OVERALL, THE PLAN WORKED PERFECTLY. HERE'S THE FILM FOR THE POLICE.
GREAT.
LISTEN, ANYTIME YOU FEEL LIKE WORKING TOGETHER AGAIN, I'M UP FOR IT. I THINK WE MAKE A REALLY GOOD TEAM.

"I THINK SO TOO, BUT..."
"I'VE GOT SOME OTHER STUFF GOING ON IN MY LIFE RIGHT NOW. I THINK I'M GOING TO HAVE TO CONCENTRATE ON IT FOR A WHILE."
CLASS SCHEDULES
GOTHAM UNIVERSITY

Oh. THAT'S TOO BAD.
I WISH THIS WASN'T THE ONLY WAY WE COULD... SEE EACH OTHER.

"YEAH. ME TOO."
21

ARE YOU SURE YOU BROUGHT ENOUGH TOWELS?! I CAN BRING SOME TOMORROW--
RELAX, DAD. I'VE GOT PLENTY. GOT TO GO NOW -- I'M LATE FOR CLASS.
CALL YOU TONIGHT.
GOTHA
UNIVERSI

ONE SUMMER VACATION AND YOU FORGET WHERE EVERY-THING IS...
CAMPUS MAP

HEY!
Oh, GREAT.

I REALIZE YOU'RE USED TO BEING DRIVEN, GRAYSON, BUT IF YOU'D WATCH WHERE YOU'RE WALKING...
Oh! AS ANOTHER ZINGER FROM GORDON FAILS TO HIT ITS MARK...
THE END

WIN ORIGINAL BATMAN ADVENTURES ART!
DETAILS INSIDE!
APPROVED BY THE COMICS CODE AUTHORITY
DC
$1.50 US
$2.00 CAN
70p UK
THE
fox kids network

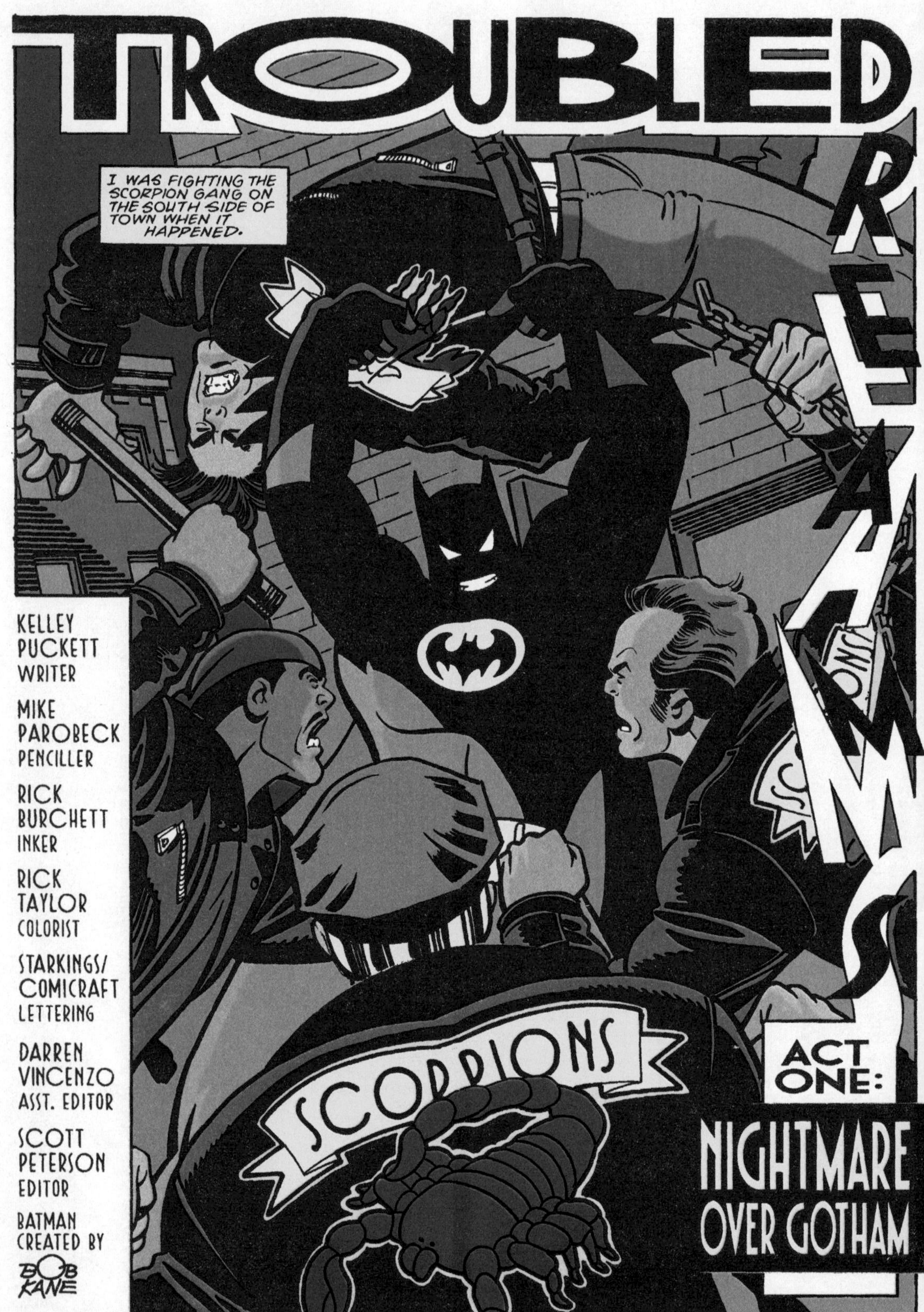
TROUBLED DREAMS
I WAS FIGHTING THE SCORPION GANG ON THE SOUTH SIDE OF TOWN WHEN IT HAPPENED.
KELLEY PUCKETT WRITER
MIKE PAROBECK PENCILLER
RICK BURCHETT INKER
RICK TAYLOR COLORIST
STARKINGS/ COMICRAFT LETTERING
DARREN VINCENZO ASST. EDITOR
SCOTT PETERSON EDITOR
BATMAN CREATED BY BOB KANE
SCORPIONS
ACT ONE:
NIGHTMARE OVER GOTHAM

APPROXIMATELY FIVE SECONDS INTO THE FIGHT THEY SUDDENLY SPOTTED SOME-THING BEHIND ME.

SOMETHING THAT SCARED THEM. I TURNED...

EXIT
...AND FROZE.

I REACTED INSTINCTIVELY AS IF FIGHTING FOR MY LIFE. AS IF THE CASTER OF THAT SHADOW SOMEHOW POSED A MORTAL THREAT.
2

WHEN SHE ROUNDED THE CORNER, THE FEAR DISSIPATED IMMEDIATELY. AS IF IT WERE JUST... CUT OFF.
WHAT'S MORE DISTURBING IS THAT EVEN NOW, EVEN HERE, I SEEM UNABLE TO COMPLETE A SKETCH OF THE SILHOUETTE.
I ... HAVE NO EXPLANATION FOR WHAT'S HAPPENING TO ME.
I'M NOT GOING OUT AGAIN TONIGHT. I'LL CONDUCT A COMPLETE SELF-EXAMINATION TOMORROW MORNING.
END OF LOG.
3

MARK OF
ZORRO
KANE BL
POPCORN!

KANE BL
5

NO!

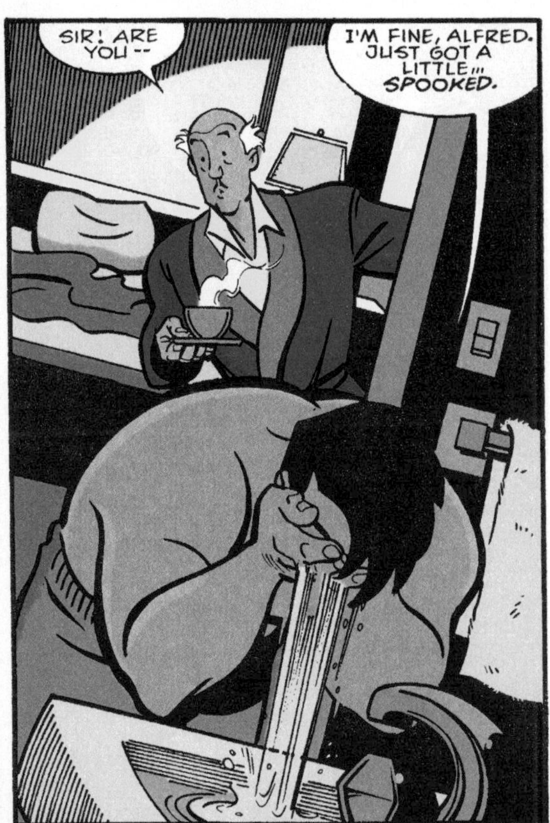
SIR! ARE YOU --
I'M FINE, ALFRED. JUST GOT A LITTLE... SPOOKED.

THAT TEA-- YOU WERE ALREADY AWAKE?
YES. I HAD THE MOST... HORRID NIGHT-MARE...

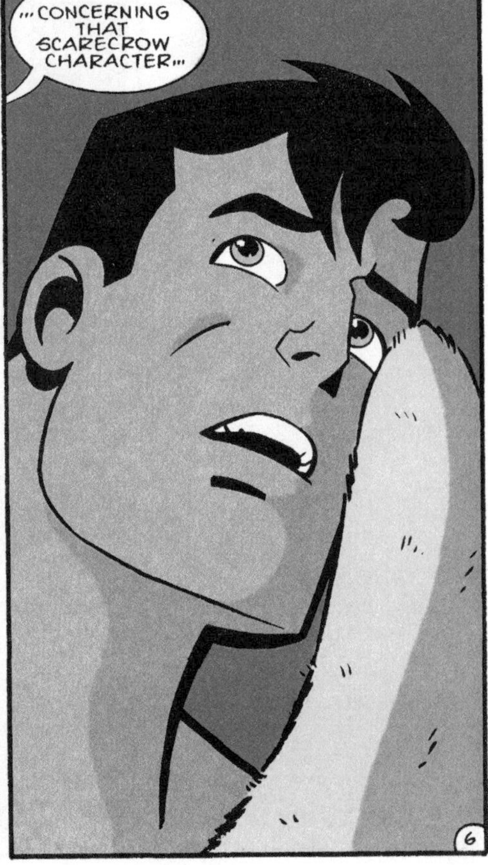
...CONCERNING THAT SCARECROW CHARACTER...
6

THERE WERE A FEW DOZEN REPORTS OF SCARECROW NIGHTMARES TWO NIGHTS AGO. LAST NIGHT, THERE WERE OVER TWELVE THOUSAND COMING IN FROM ALL OVER GOTHAM.

AND THOSE ARE JUST THE REPORTED CASES. EVERYONE I KNOW HAS HAD ONE. I DON'T SUPPOSE *YOU'VE*--
CRANE
YOU SAID CRANE PUT ON THE SCARECROW COSTUME BEFORE HE ESCAPED?

RIGHT. HE RAN IN HERE AND LOCKED THE DOOR BEHIND HIM. BY THE TIME THE ORDERLIES FORCED IT OPEN, HE WAS WEARING THE COSTUME. THEY RAN SCREAMING AND HE STROLLED OUT THE FRONT DOOR.
ANY SUGGESTIONS?

REQUEST THE NATIONAL GUARD.
IF I CAN'T STOP SCARECROW BEFORE HE APPEARS IN PUBLIC, YOU'LL HAVE A *RIOT* ON YOUR HANDS.
7

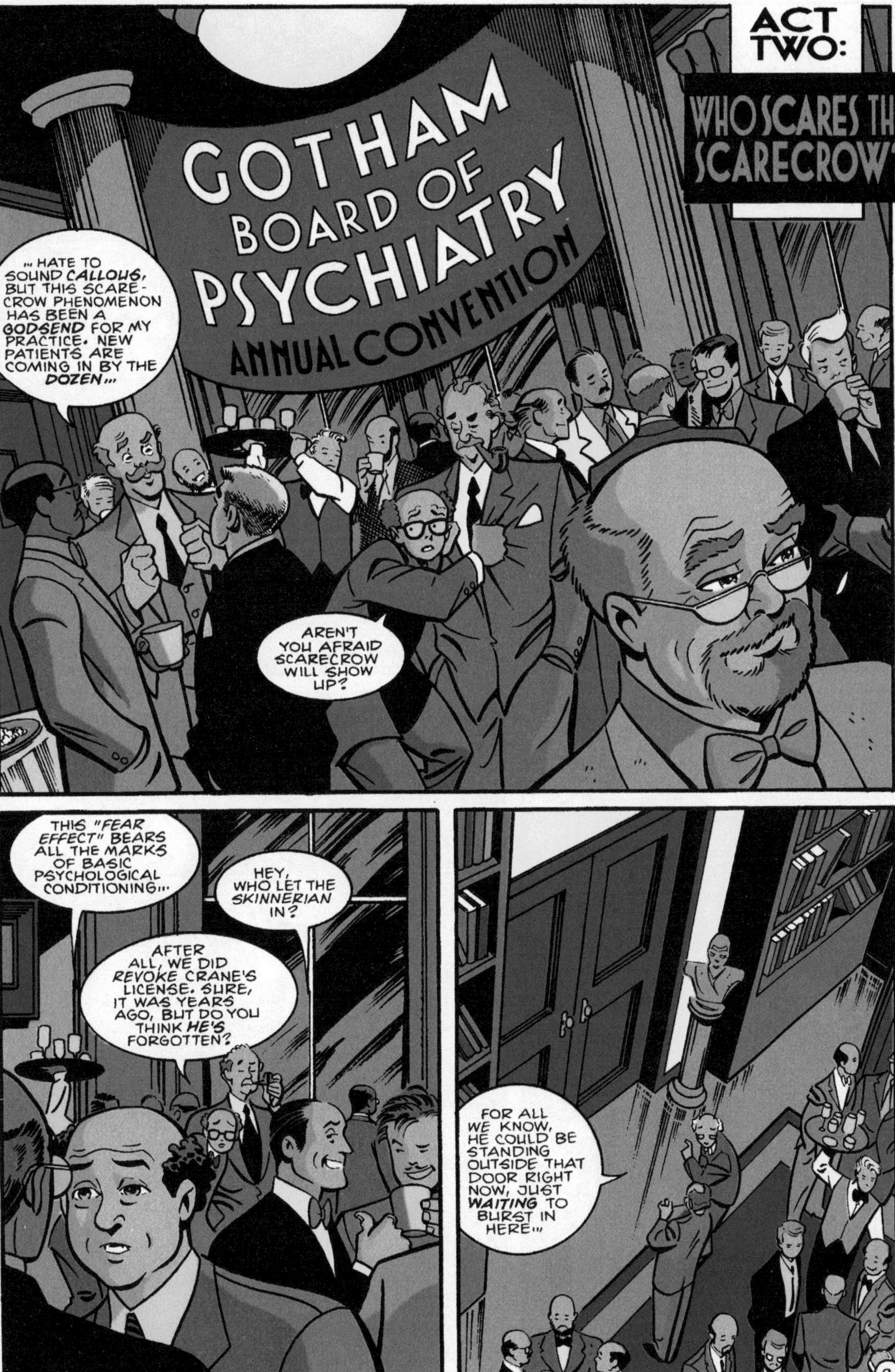

ACT TWO:

WHO SCARES THE SCARECROW?

GOTHAM BOARD OF PSYCHIATRY ANNUAL CONVENTION

... HATE TO SOUND *CALLOUS*, BUT THIS SCARECROW PHENOMENON HAS BEEN A *GODSEND* FOR MY PRACTICE. NEW PATIENTS ARE COMING IN BY THE *DOZEN*...

AREN'T YOU AFRAID SCARECROW WILL SHOW UP?

UNSUSPECTING FOOLS! LITTLE DO THEY KNOW THAT THEIR WORST NIGHTMARE IS WAITING RIGHT OUTSIDE THIS DOOR!
GIVE IT UP... SCARE-CROW.

YOU'RE... C-COMING WITH ME.
REALLY? AND WHAT'LL YOU DO IF I REFUSE -- QUIVER AT ME?

Oh, BATMAN. THE RAW FEAR GOING THROUGH YOUR SYSTEM RIGHT NOW -- IT MUST BE AMAZING. HOW LONG CAN YOU KEEP FROM RUNNING, I WONDER?
WHAT IF, FOR EXAMPLE, I WERE TO SAY...

BOO!
9

HAHAHAHA

COMIN' AT YA!

THE FEAR... GONE. COULD IT BE THAT SIMPLE?
JINGLE

OR I'LL HUFF AND I'LL PUFF...
10

... AND I'LL BLOW --
Eh?

COME ON IN AND GET ME, SCARECROW.

WHAT'S THE MATTER? AFRAID OF THE DARK?
HE KNOWS!

YAAAAAH

IT'S THE SCARECROW! RUN FOR YOUR LIVES! I'LL KILL YOU ALL!

PLEASE: LET ME THROUGH!

MOVE ASIDE!

CHEZ HALM
WHICH WAY DID HE GO?
WHICH WAY?
12

SUCCESS, SIR?
PROGRESS, ALFRED.
IT SEEMS WE'RE BEING CONDITIONED TO FEAR THE SCARECROW'S IMAGE. YOU SEE HIM, YOU BECOME AFRAID. HE LEAVES -- OR YOU STOP LOOKING AT HIM -- AND THE FEAR DISSIPATES.

AND THE NIGHTMARES?
A SIDE EFFECT? I DON'T KNOW. ALL I CAN SAY FOR SURE IS THAT SOMEHOW, SCARECROW'S GETTING HIS IMAGE INTO OUR HEADS.

BUT HOW?
I DON'T WATCH TELEVISION. MANY PEOPLE DON'T READ NEWSPAPERS. WHAT ARE WE ALL LOOKING AT?

WAIT! THAT LAST CAPER OF HIS -- THE TRANSMITTER THAT ALTERED THE SPEECH-RECOGNITION CENTER OF THE BRAIN. IT OPERATED ON THE PRINCIPLE THAT SPECIFIC AREAS OF THE BRAIN RESPOND TO HIGH-FREQUENCY TRANSMISSIONS.
13

COULD IT POSSIBLY HAVE BEEN REDESIGNED TO BEAM A SPECIFIC IMAGE *DIRECTLY* INTO OUR VISUAL CORTICES?
A SIGNAL OF THAT STRENGTH *SHOULD* BE EASILY DETECTABLE...

SURELY SUCH A CONTRAPTION IS BEYOND THE CURRENT LEVEL OF TECHNOLOGY...
WELL BEYOND. BUT SO WAS SCARECROW'S FIRST DEVICE. I DIDN'T THINK HE'D BUILT IT -- I *KNOW* HE COULDN'T HAVE BUILT *THIS* ONE.
SCANNING...

TRANSMISSION FOUND. TRACKING POINT OF ORIGIN...
GOT IT.
THANKS FOR DINNER, ALFRED.
-*Ahem*- YOU'RE WELCOME, SIR.
14

## ACT THREE: BENEATH THE MASK

EXPERIMENT? YOU INVADE PEOPLE'S MINDS, THEIR DREAMS, TURN THE ENTIRE POPULATION OF GOTHAM INTO A PANICKED MOB AND CALL IT AN EXPERIMENT?!
I WOULDN'T EXPECT A LAYMAN TO UNDER-STAND.

THE SHEER NUMBERS--DON'T YOU SEE? I HAVE A TEST GROUP OF TWO MILLION! DO YOU HAVE ANY IDEA OF THE STATISTICAL ACCURACY I CAN ACHIEVE?

THIS EXPERIMENT MUST BE COMPLETED! THERE HASN'T BEEN THIS GREAT AN OPPORTUNITY FOR DIRECT STUDY OF HUMAN SUBJECTS SINCE WORLD WAR TWO!

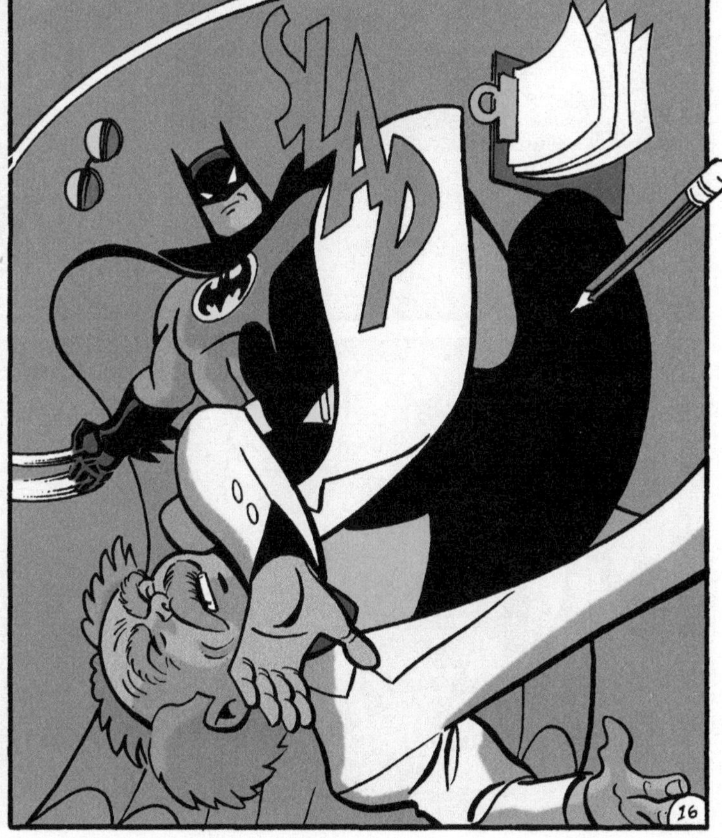
SLAP
16

HOW DO YOU FEEL *NOW? SCARED?*
REMEMBER HOW MUCH *YOU* ENJOYED IT THE NEXT TIME YOU GET A BRIGHT IDEA.

I'M SHUTTING YOUR *"EXPERIMENT"* DOWN. HOW DO I REVERSE THE CONDITIONING?
Y-YOU COULD BUILD ANOTHER MACHINE TO REVERSE THE PROCESS, B-BUT THAT WOULD TAKE *MONTHS*.

THE EFFECT WILL WEAR OFF ON ITS OWN IN TWO, THREE WEEKS.
THREE *WEEKS?* NOT GOOD ENOUGH.
SCARECROW'S STILL WALKING THE STREETS.
17

BOX JEANS
SPOT COLA
MIDAS CAMERA
AIRLINES
NOW PLAYING
HAMLET
STARRING K. CONROY
LIQUOR
RUN!

BOX JEANS
SPOT COLA
MIDAS CAMERA
AIRLINES
NOW PLAYING
HAMLET
STARRING K. CONROY
LIQUOR
SCATTER!

BOX JEANS
SPOT COLA
MIDAS CAMERA
AIRLINES
NOW PLAYING
HAMLET
STARRING K. CONROY
LIQUOR
FLEE BEFORE ME!
18

LOOK UPON MY FACE, GOTHAM!
BOX JEANS
KONY
KWA
AIRLINES
MAJESTIC THEATER
CONROY
THE FACE OF FEAR!
19

IT'S OVER, SCARE-CROW.
WHAT? HOW DID YOU--? JUST A SECOND AGO THERE WAS NOBODY --

NEVER MIND. IT DOESN'T MATTER.
NOTHING YOU CAN DO TO ME MATTERS! NO JAIL CAN HOLD ME! NO COURT CAN CONVICT ME!

WHY? BECAUSE THEY'RE ALL SCARED OF ME!
THEY'RE FINALLY ALL SCARED OF ME!
20

WRONG...

...CRANE.

THEY AREN'T SCARED OF YOU.

THEY NEVER WERE.
GOTHAM ELECTRIC
21

WELL, THINGS SEEM RELATIVELY BACK TO NORMAL.
GOTHAM GAZETTE
SCARECROW CAPTURED!
GOTHAM BREATHES EASIER
by STARSHINE ROWELL
THE FEAR EFFECT SHOULD WEAR OFF COMPLETELY WITHIN THE WEEK.
AND NOT A MOMENT TOO SOON, FOR MY TASTE. NIGHTMARES EVERY NIGHT IS NO WAY TO LIVE ONE'S LIFE.
OH, DEAR.
I DO APOLOGIZE, SIR.
THAT'S... ALL RIGHT, ALFRED.
THE END

WIN ORIGINAL BATMAN ADVENTURES ART! DETAILS INSIDE!
APPROVED BY THE COMICS CODE AUTHORITY
DC
BATMAN ADVENTURES
20 MAY 94
$1.50 US
$2.00 CAN
70p UK
THE BATMAN ADVENTURES
fox kids network
BY PUCKETT, PAROBECK & BURCHETT

SMELLS LIKE BLACK SUNDAY
BANK
APRIL 10TH: THIS LATEST CHAPTER IN MY HISTORY OF CRIMINAL PURSUITS BEGAN TWO DAYS AGO WHEN I AGREED TO REUNITE WITH MY FORMER PARTNERS, MASTERMIND AND MR. NICE.
ACT ONE
AND A PERFESSER SHALL LEAD THEM
KELLEY PUCKETT WRITER
MIKE PAROBECK PENCILLER
RICK BURCHETT INKER
RICK TAYLOR COLORIST
STARKINGS/ COMICRAFT LETTERING
DARREN VINCENZO ASST. ED.
SCOTT PETERSON EDITOR
BATMAN CREATED BY BOB KANE

ALL RIGHT, MASTERMIND, I'M IN.
GOOD. MR. NICE?
IT'LL BE TOUGH, BUT I'LL TRY.
6365476
6365472
6365473

OKAY. ANY IDEAS ON HOW WE GET OUT OF HERE, PERFESSER?
THAT SHOULDN'T BE TOO DIFFICULT. WE'LL NEED A DIVERSION, THOUGH...
Ahem.

FIRE.

BRILLIANT! WHAT NOW?
NOW WE NEED A GUN. NICE--?
2

WHAK
OW!

Oh GEEZ! DID THAT HIT YOUR FUNNY BONE? I DIDN'T MEAN TO --
CUT IT OUT, NICE! YOU PROMISED!

NOW PUT A BULLET TWENTY-EIGHT INCHES OVER AND FORTY-TWO INCHES DOWN FROM THAT CORNER UP THERE.
WHAT'S UP THERE?

BLAM
POWER LINES.
ZZZZT
3

NOW FOLLOW ME: THIRTY-FOUR PACES TO OUR RIGHT...

... NOW A LEFT TURN. AND FIFTY-SIX PACES STRAIGHT AHEAD...

... AND ANOTHER LEFT. NOW CROUCH DOWN AND MOVE FORWARD.

BONK
Ouch!
YOU WEREN'T CROUCHING!
4

AND HERE WE ARE.
AMAZING! I'M IMPRESSED...
HEY, GUYS, LOOK!

DOGGIES!

ARE THOSE ROTTWEILERS OR DOBER-MANS?
SNAP
DON'T JUST SIT THERE! SHOOT 'EM!
Huh?!
5

THWEEEEET
HEY!
SNAP

HOW COULD YOU *DO* THAT?
Oh, STOP YOUR WHINING AND LISTEN UP. HERE'S THE PLAN...

6

BLAM
BLAM
BLAM
MASTERMIND'S PLAN WAS INCOMPLETE, YET UNCHARACTERISTICALLY COMPETENT. THE STAKES WERE HIGH, BUT SUCCESS WOULD GIVE US POWER OVER THE ENTIRE EASTERN SEABOARD.
FOR THE FIRST TIME IN RECENT MEMORY, MASTERMIND HAD COME UP WITH A SCHEME THAT JUST MIGHT WORK.
OF PARTICULAR INTEREST WAS THE ENDGAME, WHICH I PLAYED NO SMALL PART IN DEVISING. IN SIMPLE TERMS, THE PLAN...
WHAP
THUNK
HA! DIDN'T THINK I'D PLAN ON NEEDING STEEL-REINFORCED TIRES, Eh?
AMATEUR!
Hm. I'VE GONE BLANK.
WHAT WAS THE PLAN AGAIN, MASTERMIND?
ENOUGH WITH THE MEMOIRS, ALREADY! IT'S TIME FOR SOME ACTION!
7

# ACT TWO: FLYING BLIND WITH MASTERMIND

BUT SERIOUSLY, WHAT'S THIS TIMER FOR? AND WHY DO YOU HAVE THE POLICE BAND PLAY --
QUIET! I REQUIRE SILENCE!
DO YOU HAVE ANY IDEA OF THE COMPLEXITIES INVOLVED HERE?! DO YOU?

I'VE DEVISED A ROUTE THAT WILL ENABLE ME TO SUSTAIN A SPEED OF NINETY MILES PER HOUR THROUGHOUT ALL OF GOTHAM CITY WITHOUT HITTING ONE RED LIGHT!
NOT ONE!
BANK
BATMAN
1RST AVE
POLICE
BASE
HQ

QUITE IMPRESSIVE, MASTERMIND, BUT HE IS STARTING TO GAIN ON US...
WELL THEN! TIME TO CUT ONE CLOSE AND SEE WHAT HE'S MADE OF!
9

HOPE YOU GOT INSURANCE, BAT-BOY!

NITROUS OXIDE: ENGAGED

AH, NITROUS OXIDE. SURE BRINGS BACK MEMORIES...
THREE MINUTES LEFT! SHUT UP AND TAKE THE WHEEL!

HELP! POLICE! THERE'S A CRAZY MAN WITH A GUN! HE'S SHOOTING EVERYBODY!
BLAM
BLAM
CORNER OF TIMM AND RADOMSKI! Oh, THE HUMANITY!

KELLEY'S PUB
ALL UNITS IN THE VICINITY OF TIMM AND RADOMSKI RESPOND IMMEDIATELY... SHOOTING IN PROGRESS...

CAR FIFTY-FOUR RESPONDING... PROCEEDING ALONG BROADWAY...
BINGO!
BANK
BATMAN
11

RIGHT ON TIME!
EOOOEEE

EEEOOOE
SCREEECH

12

HERE, NOW YOU CALL ONE IN.
I THINK WE HAVE A PROBLEM.
0:55
WHAT!?
NOOO!
THWEET THWEET
HAWS
DEPARTMENT STORE
AAAAAHHHHHK!
13

WELL, **HE** SURE CAUGHT UP IN A HURRY.
Huh?

C'MON BABY
C'MON BABY
C'MON BABY
0:05
FIVE...

...FOUR...

...THREE... TWO...
YOU'RE COMING WITH ME.
0:02

...ONE... ZERO! ZERO, BATMAN! KNOW WHAT THAT MEANS?
YOU'RE TOO LATE!
TOO LATE FOR WHAT?
15

AT THIS VERY MOMENT, MR. NICE IS BEGINNING HIS ASSAULT ON THE FORT BRIGGS COMPOUND! YOU KNOW, THE ONE WITH THE WARHEADS?!.
BEFORE THE DAY IS OUT, I'LL BE A NUCLEAR POWER!

AND AS OF FIFTEEN SECONDS AGO, THERE'S NO MEANS OF TRANS-PORTATION ON EARTH THAT COULD GET YOU THERE IN TIME TO STOP HIM!
HE'LL SLICE THROUGH THEIR DEFENSES LIKE A HOT KNIFE --

MR. NICE? WHAT MAKES YOU THINK HE WON'T STOP HIMSELF BEFORE HE HURTS ANYONE?
BECAUSE, BAT-BOY, I MADE HIM PROMISE TO STOP BEING NICE UNTIL MIDNIGHT TONIGHT! AND NOW, IF YOU'LL EXCUSE ME...

I'M A NUCLEAR POW-ER! I'M A NUCLEAR POW-ER
MAYBE TELLING HIM WASN'T SUCH A GOOD IDEA.
JIM. LISTEN CARE-FULLY...
16

# ACT LEGEND OF THE DARK NICE

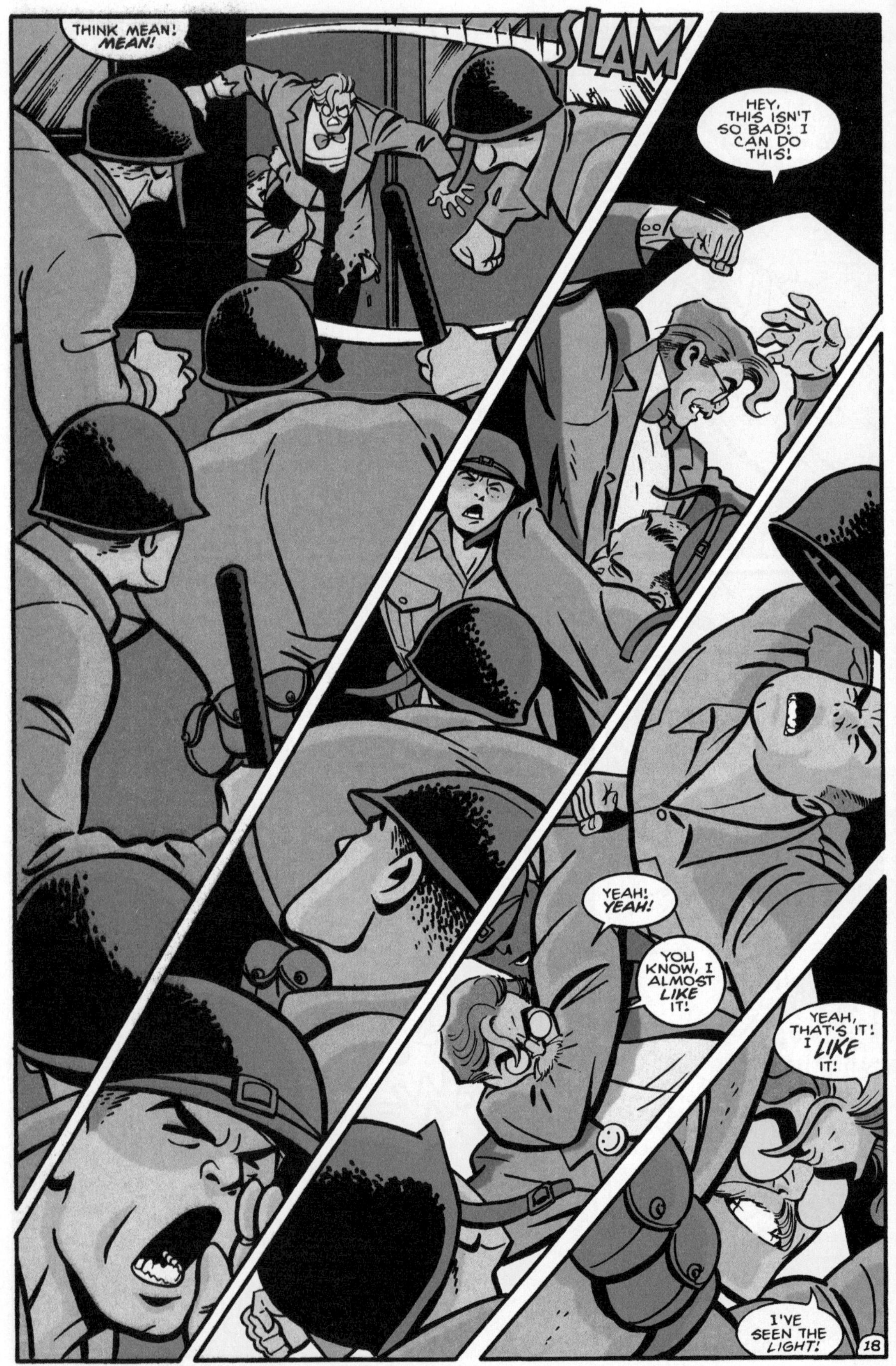
THINK MEAN! MEAN!
SLAM
HEY, THIS ISN'T SO BAD! I CAN DO THIS!
YEAH! YEAH!
YOU KNOW, I ALMOST LIKE IT!
YEAH, THAT'S IT! I LIKE IT!
I'VE SEEN THE LIGHT!
18

NO MORE MR. NICE GUY!

HAHAHA

HAHAHA

BRAKATA

19

AUTHORIZED PERSONNEL ONLY
A-HA! MY TARGET IS WITHIN MY GRASP!
GOD HELP WHO-EVER'S ON THE OTHER SIDE OF THIS DOOR!

KRASH
DESPAIR! DESPAIR! THE DARK NICE COMETH!

Eh?

ARF

DANGER
UH... NOW... YOU JUST MOVE ASIDE, THERE, BOY. LET ME PASS AND THERE'LL...
...THERE'LL BE NO TROUBLE, OKAY..?

ARF!

MOVE ASIDE, NOW. DON'T MAKE ME USE THIS...

ARF?

ARF ARF

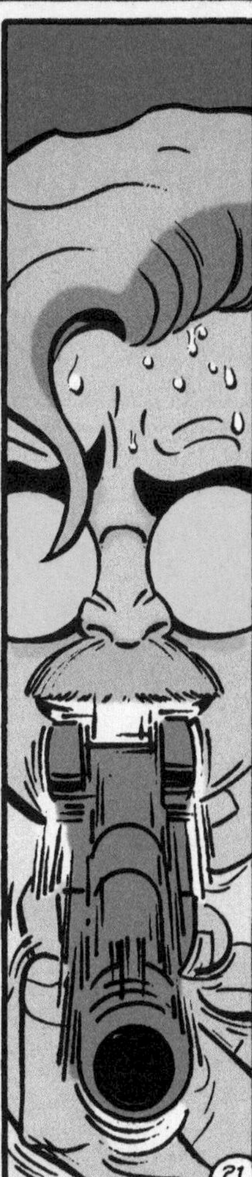
21

WHAT COULD I DO? HE WAS THE SWEETEST LITTLE FELLA...
Oh, JUST SHUT UP!
...IGNOMINIOUS DEFEAT!

BOTH OF YOU, LISTEN UP! I'VE COME UP WITH ANOTHER PLAN, AND THIS ONE'S FOOLPROOF!
THESE MASHED POTATOES REPRESENT THE GOTHAM BANKING SYSTEM, OKAY? NOW --

SORRY, I...I'M JUST NOT UP TO IT. I NEED TO BE ALONE FOR A WHILE.
COUNT ME OUT, TOO. I'VE GOT A DATE WITH A PUBLISHER.

SO I'M FLYING SOLO, Eh? FINE! SWEET VENGEANCE WILL BE MINE AND MINE ALONE!
DO YOU HEAR ME, GOTHAM?! ARE YOU TREMBLING?!

APPARENTLY NOT.
TRASH
THE END